NECK AND BACK PROBLEMS

NECK and BACK PROBLEMS
THE SPINE AND RELATED DISORDERS

JAN DE VRIES

From the BY APPOINTMENT ONLY series

MAINSTREAM
PUBLISHING

First published in 1987 by
MAINSTREAM PUBLISHING CO. (EDINBURGH) LTD.
7 Albany Street
Edinburgh EH1 3UG

ISBN 1 85158 084 0 (cloth)
ISBN 1 85158 083 2 (paper)

British Library Cataloguing in Publication Data
De Vries, Jan, 1937—
  Back and neck problems: the spine and related disorders.—
  (By appointment only).
  1. Spine — Wounds and injuries
  I. Title II. Series
  617'.48206   RD533
  ISBN 1-85158-084-0
  ISBN 1-85158-083-2 Pnl

Typeset in 11/12 Palatino by Mainstream Publishing.
Printed in Great Britain by Collins, Glasgow.

Contents

Books available from the same author in the
By Appointment Only series:

Stress and Nervous Disorders (third edition)

Multiple Sclerosis

Traditional Home and Herbal Remedies

Arthritis, Rheumatism and Psoriasis (second edition)

Do Miracles Exist?

Preface

I FEEL HONOURED and complimented to write the Preface to Jan de Vries' new book on the spine. We have known each other for many years.

In entering into the study of this book, let things of the past be past. This book is one with a look to the future, and is for those who shall live for the future.

The spine (spinal column) is the 'telephone exchange' for the functions of the whole human body, and is therefore one of the most important factors to life and health. In this modern world most of us seem to abuse the spine (ie the back) and consequently to suffer from the present day disease — low backache — which is usually caused by abnormal posture.

Let the motto of this book be summed up in the following words: *'normal structure produces normal function'*.

I wish this book all the success it deserves, and may the reading public find something within its pages to help them along, and ease their suffering.

Leonard J. Allan, DO, ND, Dr(Ac)
Margate
Kent
England

1

The Spine and Spinal Cord

OVER THE MANY years that I have been in practice I have seen so many patients who, in one way or another, are troubled with problems related to the spine or spinal column. Some suffer acute pain, while others are chronically affected. Yet the suffering of most of these patients can often be reduced, minimised or even cured with the application of the correct treatment.

In this book I hope to explain some of these problems and, although I have undergone extensive training, as time has gone on I have developed many of my own methods in dealing with these complaints. It is with gratitude that I look through the many testimonials I have received, and must conclude that some of these methods have brought relief to many back sufferers and to people suffering from other conditions, the cause of which may be traced to the spine.

The disorders discussed in this book are not specifically confined to modern times, but have been present in mankind for centuries. Nevertheless it seems they have recently become more common. A possible reason for this may be a general lack of exercise, although faulty nutrition may also be to blame. Incorrect dietary management may well be a possible cause for these ailments, which can be so crippling.

Many books have been written on this subject, but the reader may find that my approach differs from that of many of my colleagues, because through my long experience I have developed my own methods which have proven successful. These may also be adapted to the needs of individual patients, as flexibility both in diagnosing the source of the problem and the appropriate treatment is of prime importance.

First of all we should know that the spinal column comprises 33 vertebrae and is divided into five different sections:

- —the neck or the cervical vertebrae, consisting of seven vertebrae;
- —the chest, dorsal or thoracic vertebrae, consisting of twelve vertebrae;
- —the lower back or lumbar vertebrae, consisting of five vertebrae;
- —the sacrum, consisting of five fused vertebrae;
- —the tail of the spine or coccyx, consisting of four small vertebrae, which almost resemble crystals.

Between each of the vertebrae of the neck, chest and back is a small disc or pad of fibrous tissue. These intervertebral discs act as a buffer or cushion between the bones.

The spine houses and protects the spinal cord, which is the nerve tissue of the central nervous system. This ranges from the atlas — the topmost vertebra of the neck — to the lower border of the first, or upper, border of the second lumbar area. It is connected with the brain and extends to the first segment of the coccyx.

The condition of the spinal column is subject to the ageing process of man and so alters through the different stages of life. Its properties vary as does the function of each vertebra. Basically, it protects the spinal cord, which conducts messages to and from the brain. There is also a watery fluid which we know as the cerebrospinal fluid, protecting the cord as well as the brain, and this acts as a fluid cushion.

Therefore, when talking about the spinal cord, we should also look into the nervous system. This complicated system can be divided into two parts, the central nervous system and the peripheral or autonomic nervous system.

The brain contained in the skull has long nerve fibres or pathways which transmit messages to the body. These nerves or fibres pass down the centre of the spinal column in a central channel and then out between each vertebra, where they divide into a motor part and an autonomic part.

The motor part of the nerve supplies the voluntary muscles and the autonomic part aids the body with all the autonomic functions which take place involuntarily, for example, blinking of the eyes, breathing and digestion.

The nervous system is built up of a variety of nervous tissue and presents an osteopath with a wide choice when treating a patient. The diagram on page 15 makes this clear. If everything is working in harmony, there is no trouble. If not, however, it is like throwing a pebble into the water — where the pebble lands is not important, but the resulting ripples may have unforeseen results!

I am sure that the Italian physician Luigi Galvani (1737-98) would have been in agreement. He discovered that a frog's calf muscles could be made to contract when the nerve to this muscle was prodded with two pins of different metals. In this way a weak electric current was induced, which caused a response in the muscle tissue, resulting in a muscular contraction.

Let us consider that, of the 43 pairs of nerves belonging to the nervous system, 31 are spinal nerves, ie are connected with the spinal cord, and 12 pairs are cranial nerves, ie are connected with the brain.

Galvani discovered that stimulating the motor nerve immediately resulted in a muscular contraction. Although the muscle and the nerve are not directly connected, they do have meeting points called synapses. Neuro-physiologists have since discovered that contraction will take place through changes in the muscle tissue membrane.

We should not underestimate the importance of the minerals potassium and sodium for a healthy nervous system. The autonomic nervous system is a motor or a supplier to the muscle and glands. These are divided into the sympathetic and para-sympathetic systems. The sympathetic nervous system has sympathetic cells in the spinal cord as well as in the chest. The nerves of the para-sympathetic system originate in the sacral cord and in the brain. The para-sympathetic system is called into action when the body is under stress, eg fear or flight. Usually the para-sympathetic system works in opposition to the sympathetic nervous system.

Nerve cells cannot be replaced and after the age of 25 the nervous system begins to degenerate, hence the importance of a correct diet. I want to take this opportunity to stress a point which I never fail to tell students at their seminars: osteopathy and naturopathy should always go hand in hand.

Osteopathy is a system of medicine which places its chief emphasis on the relationship between structural integrity and health. The body is endowed with the means of sustaining optimum health, but this may be impaired by mechanical defects. Gross defects usually come within the category of orthopaedic lesions, although the osteopathic lesion may in itself be very minor and difficult to detect. Frequently, such lesions are nothing more than loss of joint tolerance, which may give rise to joint pain and limitation of movement.

Although osteopathy is most often used for treating muscular or skeletal problems, it is also employed effectively for other disorders. It is well established that manipulation of the spine can alter neuro-endocrine and neuro-visceral activity and thus affect general health. Therefore a good osteopath will always regard the vascular system as being of prime importance and employ a fair amount of soft tissue manipulation.

10

Naturopathy, however, deals mainly with the life force. It recognises that this force may be stimulated by fasting, correct dieting, restoration of structural integrity, hydrotherapy and exercise.

More than a century ago, the American country doctor, Andrew T. Still, learned how closely these methods were related and of their influence on problems stemming from the spinal column. Having worked with patients for a long time, he realised that harmony could be re-established between muscles, nerves and other vital parts of the human body. By soft tissue manipulation and influencing the patient's lifestyle he even recorded successes with gall bladder problems and gallstones. As a result, this manual therapy aroused the interest of the academic world and, when it was shown on X-ray that disalignments could easily be corrected, osteopathy came into its own.

After the Second World War various tests proved that artificial osteopathic lesions could be induced by injecting a simple salt solution. A difference in breathing and heart rhythm was produced. A well-trained osteopath will soon realise when problems originate from the spine and, with gentle manipulation or palpation, will locate the area of trouble. After he has relaxed the muscles he will be able to bring about the right adjustment by simple pressure.

However, an osteopath or manipulative therapist requires in-depth knowledge of the skeleton. He must know how to interpret X-rays accurately and cannot afford to take any risks. He needs to work carefully, especially where osteopathic lesions are strains of body tissue.

When a joint is involved, the ligaments are primarily affected, so the term ligamentous articular strain applies. The ligaments of the joints are normally in a balanced tension and seldom, if ever, are they completely relaxed throughout the normal range of movements. The lesion is produced by over-balance of the reciprocal tension of those ligaments which have not been strained. This tends to lock the articular mechanism and prevent its free and normal movement. It is

11

the ligaments which are primarily involved in the origin of the lesion and not the muscular leverage.

The articulation is carried in the direction of the lesion, so exaggerating it. This causes the tension of the weakened ligaments to be equal to, or slightly in excess of, the tension of those that are not strained. When this tension is properly balanced, the respiratory and muscular co-operation of the patient is employed to overcome the resistance of the body's defence mechanism to the release of the lesion.

This does not need severe manipulation (as is so often, and unnecessarily, done). The body's natural tendency is always to want to revert to normal, once the balance is restored. With some simple breathing exercises it is sometimes surprising how the normal balance restores the disalignment.

Osteopathic techniques are not homogenous, as new techniques are daily introduced into practice, and analysis has taught us that many people find benefit in these methods. In fact, even though we speak of osteopathic techniques, in principle these do not exist. Manipulative methods depend on the practitioner, who should be well trained to work with the human body. In the years that I have been working in this field I have developed my own methods in trying to help my patients. Such treatment should never be violent, but administered in a gentle way to get the desired result.

An old friend of mine in Germany once said: 'Osteopaths are born and not created!' He may have a point there. A correct diagnosis and a subtle approach are required. Thorough inspection of the spine is essential and, by its movements, the whereabouts of the affected area can soon be discovered. This is one of the reasons why 'bone setters' in olden days were often so successful. They were generally gifted in finding the troubled spot and managed to correct it. However, they occasionally did cause harm due to their lack of basic knowledge of the spinal column.

The art of medicine reaches back into prehistoric days and is instinctive, since even animals, given the chance, will treat their own ills. Instinct tells them to lick their wounds and eat healing herbs. They will also keep a broken limb in a protected position. From old scrolls, found in Egypt and Peru, it has been found that the principles of massage and manipulation are as old as mankind.

In 1874, when Dr Andrew T. Still reached the point that he realised what he had discovered, he named it 'osteopathy', derived from the Greek word *osteon*, meaning bone or bones. Later, Dr D. D. Palmer, from Harvey Lillet (USA), called his methods 'chiropractic' treatment, which is based on the Greek word *cheir*, meaning hand.

However, as I have already mentioned, osteopathic manipulative treatment is not synonymous with chiropractic methods. Newer techniques have modified today's treatment and the spine and spinal problems can be treated in many ways, some of which will be described in this book.

Again I will stress the importance of a properly balanced diet. Dietetic requirements are equally important as physical exercise. A deficient diet reduces oxygenation of the body tissue and the production of energy, thereby undermining the immune system. The influence of diet on the spinal cord is therefore significant.

I have often wondered why so many young people in the age group of 25 to 35 years old seem to have spinal problems. My conclusion is that it may be due to physical demands, coupled with insufficient knowledge of, or attention to, nutrition. We may well find the origin of so many spinal complaints here.

Nerve activity is essential, ie transporting nutritional substance to the cells through the blood stream. Muscle cells will not contract, nor will gland cells secrete, without nerve impulses. The nerve impulses are responsible for the function of the cells, and muscular contractions and glandular secretion depends on the correct functioning of the nervous system.

With these principles in mind, the osteopath's treatment will help to rebuild the immune system, which is subjected to many adverse influences. The object of treatment is to remove the causative factor as far as this is possible, thus controlling the symptoms and restoring the functions of the patient. Of course, hereditary factors should not be overlooked and it is not claimed that every ailment will respond to treatment and be remedied. This depends largely on what caused the patient's problem in the first place.

The role of the blood must definitely not be underestimated and deserves our full care and attention in order to facilitate the correct functioning of a healthy spinal cord.

We have seen that the spinal cord is part of the central nervous system in the spine and contains many nerve cells and bundles of nerve fibres which connect various levels of the spinal cord with the brain. Modern society creates adverse influences on the central nervous system, thus making us more susceptible to viruses, infections and inflammations.

In subsequent chapters I intend to discuss individual parts of the spinal column. We will study these and their different functions separately and look into the aspects of treatment, prevention and self-help methods.

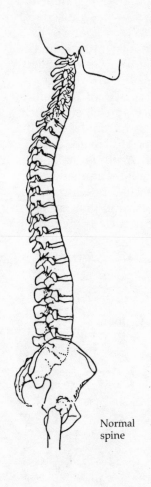

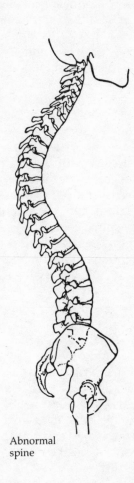

Normal
spine

Abnormal
spine

2

The Cervical Spine

THE CERVICAL SPINE is divided into two distinct areas:

> —the upper part, consisting of two vertebrae, namely the
> atlas and the axis;
> —the lower part, consisting of five vertebrae.

The head may weigh as much as 25 lbs and therefore the muscles and neck joints must function very precisely, in order to balance the weight of the head. The neck and the vertebrae are in a forward curvature and the muscles can be compared to the ropes of a sailing ship. If the muscles and joints do not support the head correctly, pains in the neck or arm are often the result.

Painful necks are frequently due to a poor posture. Many problems also occur as a result of incorrect movements or incorrect exercises, while car accidents are often the cause of whiplash injuries.

The kind of neck problems due to poor posture could also flare up as a result of a simple cough or sneeze. Moreover, we should realise that postural changes take place over a period of time. A good example of this is the typist who works at her desk for long stretches in a static position. Many people, too, are guilty of not taking enough exercise. Whatever the cause may be, the spine should be looked after so that each vertebra can perform its normal function.

Degeneration can take place, causing the vertebrae to cease functioning properly and arthritic conditions may also put undue pressure on the spinal nerves. Cranial nerve problems, such as dizziness, ringing in the ears, or blurred vision, can occur as a result of pressure on the nerve. All these symptoms can usually be traced back to irregularities in the cervical spine.

Unusual movement may be the cause of pain. Tingling feelings in the fingers or arms, like a sort of numbness, or a loss of balance, tiredness or depression may also result. It is therefore of the greatest importance that good movement of the neck be maintained. This can be encouraged by exercises, palpation or manipulation. An experienced practitioner will know which action to advise.

In this chapter I will relate some of my experiences with patients where adjustment of the spine has brought relief for diverse ailments. How often do we hear it said that someone has a headache? A headache is like an alarm bell, warning us that something is not quite right. It could be a signal pointing to problems elsewhere in the body, but more often than not it signifies a spinal malfunction, usually in the cervical area.

When a headache occurs frequently, it is advisable to have it looked into. It may be caused by tension or a metabolic disorder, but could also be an indication of a more serious irregularity. In practice I have found that headaches can often be relieved by simple manipulation.

One of my patients had become incapacitated due to a slipped disc in the lumbar spine. I went over the whole of the spine and gave her manipulative treatment, which instantly brought some measure of relief. At her next visit she told me that the headaches she had suffered for so many years, had completely disappeared. She had never realised that these may have originated from her neck. The practitioner will often discover that either a dorsal or cervical disc is out of alignment and this can be rectified during treatment, as was the case with this lady. The practitioner's satisfaction in his work can hardly be measured against the gratitude of the patient.

Because of the neck's mobility, the danger is always present that displacement of one or more of the vertebrae can cause compression or irritation of the cervical nerves. The migraine type of headache is particularly distressing for the sufferer and minor irritations will affect the cranial nerves, when a dull nagging pain will often result.

A headache, therefore, can be an indication of diverse irregularities and if it occurs on a regular basis, there is little point in treating it with a painkiller or an aspirin. It is the cause of the headache which should be investigated. Fortunately, in many cases a variety of techniques, methods or remedies are available to correct the situation.

The so-called 'slipped disc lesion' in the cervical spine is not as common as in the lumbar spine, but when problems arise in the upper spine, cervical discs 2/3, 3/4 and 4/5 are usually involved. Frequently, when these discs overlap, discomfort may be experienced. A prolapsed disc can lead to a persistent pain, either at the base of the neck or on the sides. If the nerve is under pressure, the muscles which it supplies often go into spasm and this causes pain. This, of course, could affect the arms and in more serious cases could actually cause a 'drop wrist'.

One of the worst cases of a slipped disc lesion between the base of the skull and cervical 1 that I have ever come across was during one of my lectures abroad. The occasion was a lecture in St Catharine, Canada. At the front of the audience sat a girl in a wheelchair, who seemed to be listening very attentively to my lecture. Once in a while, however, when my eyes fell on her, I got the impression of a pained look on her face.

When I was in the process of winding up the lecture, I heard a sudden scream and the girl fainted. As the hall was packed with people it was virtually impossible for me to leave the platform, but I saw that a colleague of mine immediately took charge and the girl was wheeled out. When I had finished the lecture I asked the audience to wait for a moment with their questions, so that I could have an opportunity to check on the girl first.

A diagnosis was reached very quickly indeed. She had been listening carefully, with her neck craned in one position. Being prone to neck problems and because she had been sitting in the same position during most of the evening, a cervical disc had become disaligned and she had collapsed from the resulting pressure and pain. My colleague had managed to bring her round and she then said that she felt dizzy and experienced a feeling as if the blood had drained from her head. This I hear frequently from patients.

This had all combined to cause a restriction in her circulation and between us, my colleague and I soon managed to relieve her pain. These symptoms, however, often do occur if cervical problems are neglected. In her case, though, it was largely due to a degenerative condtion.

Wherever I go I always carry some Arnica in my pocket, which is tremendously useful on occasions like this. We administered some to the girl and, with the further use of some ice cubes, the pain was soon reduced and the disc was put right. The pressure in such cases may become intolerable and severe pain will extend over the occiput or the back of the head. The arteries are then under compression and the disturbance of the blood flow from the veins will give a degree of cerebral disorder which may affect the vision.

When the girl had described her symptoms of dizziness and nausea, a diagnosis was quickly reached, for which no X-rays were necessary. In similar cases the recommendation will often be a surgical collar. However, if we remember that the muscular spasms are caused by pressure on the nerve roots, we may be pleased to learn that there are less obvious methods than a collar which will sort out these problems. The strengthening remedy Araniforce, from Vogel & Weber, can be of great help if taken, and the muscles can be toned up with some physiotherapy.

The neck's mobility and the cervical spine are under considerable pressure because of the stress of modern life. Strain, wear and tear of the ligamentous and capsular structures might cause some low grade inflammation. Eventually this could lead to osteoarthritis. This does not necessarily have to result in degeneration of these structures, because an excellent homoeopathic remedy is available to us, called Symphosan and developed by Dr Vogel. This will stave off excessive degenerative damage.

Cervical muscle contraction with resulting pain is a frequent complaint. Very often, when the cervical vertebrae are so affected, neck or shoulder movement may be impaired. Tenderness of the muscles covering the spinal processes can cause spasms in the lateral and interior neck muscles. Localised muscle spasms in areas of referred pain can also be present.

For pain relief in these cases we may use acupuncture treatment, and here I have devised my own combination where I apply neural therapy, which will immediately ease the muscle spasms. This particular part of the treatment gives the patient fast pain relief.

It is in this context that I feel that the 'whiplash' injury should also be mentioned. This injury may result from a severe jolting, forwards and backwards, of the neck. Mention of a whiplash injury is invariably in connection with road accidents and collisions.

If a patient's complaints point to a whiplash injury, X-ray photographs should immediately be taken to find out if this is indeed the case. We know that people with a whiplash injury suffer real pain and discomfort and it is usually not too difficult to diagnose, especially if X-rays are available.

Such an injury may not become immediately apparent and a correct diagnosis is most important because of the many legal consequences of prolonged, or even permanent, after-effects of a car collision. Statistically, it is claimed that in every city with a population of 100,000 or over, an average of ten car accidents are reported daily. Whiplash diagnosis should, if possible, be made between 24 and 48 hours after the accident.

When the victim displays cuts and bruises these should be taken care of first and X-rays may be omitted if no neck problems are apparent. Even X-rays are not an infallible method of diagnosing whiplash. Besides, the effects of whiplash are sometimes more far-reaching than an X-ray may give credit for. Many whiplash injuries are still the result of a dislike or aversion to wearing seat-belts, hence the American saying: 'Don't get caught dead sitting on top of your seat belts!'

It is surprising to see that most whiplash injuries result in lower-back problems. When a whiplash is diagnosed between the third and fourth cervical vertebra, it very often results in problems in the area of the fourth and fifth lumbar vertebra.

A young girl, who came to our clinic after having been injured in a fight, displayed all the symptoms of whiplash. On being told this, she remarked that she had never heard of a whiplash injury and therefore I tried to explain it to her. This is sometimes rather difficult to do in layman's terms, but I suppose that the easiest way to explain it is to try and imagine that literally everything under the head and neck has been knocked and shaken about. Sometimes, because of an acute injury, there is inflammation and in severe cases the damage can even lead to metabolic disorders.

Trying to explain the situation to the girl, I quoted the case of a middle-aged lady who had been the victim of a car collision. It was not thought too serious and she received the usual treatment for cuts and bruises. However, she then complained of bouts of dizziness and nausea and after a few days it was considered necessary to hospitalise her as she also complained of severe headaches.

Quite some time later, when visiting our clinic, she told me her story. I took some X-rays and these showed that she still had some soft tissue injuries, mainly at the base of her neck. Some blood vessels were damaged and the normal flow of

21

blood to the brain was restricted. Here we had a clear case of a brain function disorder, because she had lost her sense of smell and taste, suffered restricted shoulder movement, impaired focusing of the eyes and her speech was slightly slurred.

The above goes to show that even X-rays do not always show the severity of the injury. In this patient's case lengthy treatment was necessary before these complaints were cleared up and I prescribed some remedies, ie Araniforce, Symphosan and Urticalcin, to be followed up with acupuncture treatment.

Fortunately, most cervical problems can be remedied, especially if acute, as most whiplash injuries are. Some, however, have been the cause of such trauma that little can be achieved.

A gentleman came to the clinic with a severe cervical whiplash, which had been totally neglected. He had not been able to find the necessary help previously. He ought to have listened to the advice of his doctors, however, but he had tried to overcome his problems with a collar. The cause of these problems had been diagnosed as a herniated, ruptured, or prolapsed intervertebral disc. This can result in severe problems, because the inner nucleus pulposus protrudes from between the vertebrae and causes pressures on the nerves. Degeneration had taken place, and the pain and agony he had undergone had left him very much weakened. He had also lost a lot of hair and, when I saw him, his nails were almost black. When I examined him, I found that the reflexes of the nerve roots were depressed, neck flexion was still very painful, and there was much cervical cord compression.

I have already mentioned that he had had some help, which he had mostly ignored, however, and that he had neglected the after-care. In doing so, he had caused himself much discomfort, some of it unnecessary. Furthermore, some of the damage was by then irreparable.

The laser treatment I submitted him to was helpful and I also prescribed a calcium/silicium preparation together with Dr Vogel's Symphosan and Petasan, which often works wonders as a cell renewer. He obtained considerable relief from the pain, and we managed to get most of his problems under control, although the after-effects of the neglect will never totally disappear. It is worth remembering, as this case shows, that these particular symptoms always should be given the best of attention.

Contrary to popular thought, vertigo cannot always be ascribed to high blood pressure or hypertension, but can also be caused by cervical root syndromes, which might cause weakness, pain or sensory loss. The symptoms resemble those of vertigo, but simple manipulation together with some specific homoeopathic remedies, can be very helpful.

From personal experience I can tell about an unfortunate mishap which occurred when I was giving osteopathic treatment to a patient. It concerned a strong, well-built farmer of around 20 stone, who suffered with back and neck problems. I had to resort to some very old-fashioned osteopathic manipulation and I realised that the patient was not paying attention to my instructions. He did not fully co-operate and I suddenly felt my arm being jerked under his weight and I sensed that my own neck was in real trouble. I suspected that cervical 3/4 had to be readjusted and as I was not able to get help immediately, it affected my shoulder and arm considerably. I knew that there was a lesion and immediately took some Arnica, otherwise this cervical lesion might also affect the spinal cord and roots. I had hardly any movement left in my arm and decided to have some high frequency Diapulse treatment. I also took some homoeopathic remedies and tried some gentle massage, which of course was not easy.

Thank goodness, though, for the laser treatment, which I had only just imported from Germany. The pain was relieved to such an extent that I was able to continue work. This was so important, because I had many patients waiting for consultation and treatment. From personal experience I had now come to understand the discomfort people can suffer due to cervical lesions and disalignments.

Once, after having lectured in the Netherlands, first to practitioners and then followed by a public lecture, I arrived quite late at night to stay with friends, who were actually ex-neighbours of mine. They were very kind and fully understood that I was tired. Not long after my arrival there, however, the telephone rang and someone begged for help in connection with their daughter. It sounded sufficiently serious for me to decide to go and see them.

The distressed parents told me that their daughter had been thrown while out riding her horse. The diagnosis had been a cervical thoracic hernia, which needed immediate surgery. She had remained unconscious for more than eight weeks and the doctors could not understand the reason for this.

The diagnosis of a cervical thoracic hernia had been correct and as such the spinal cord suffered acute compression, so immediate surgery had definitely been necessary. However, the girl's condition had remained extremely poor and the parents did not know where to turn, so they asked for my opinion.

Unfortunately I was not in a position that night to see the girl, but after having had the whole situation explained to me in detail, I advised as to how the unconscious condition might possibly be overcome. I suggested to the parents that their daughter should be given brain enzyme injections, i.e. Coliacron, which is actually produced in the Netherlands. I also recommended some homoeopathic remedies and together these indeed produced the required results. The girl's improvement was sudden and surprisingly speedy. Her reflexes returned and later, when I enquired, I was informed that her condition had improved greatly. However, it was quite some time before she totally regained her strength.

I never tire of stressing the point that neck problems need expert treatment. I always repeat the warning that incorrect neck manipulations can result in more harm than good. Treatment should always be left to experienced scientific practitioners. Any neck manipulations should be knowledgeably done and let us never fail to realise that we are dealing with the finest designs The Creator has entrusted us with.

Exercises during and after recovery from neck complications should be done with the greatest care and need to be explained to patients as clearly as possible, so that they are aware of the importance of following the advice given. This is especially the case if tenderness remains in the deep muscles and spinous processes and pain is still present, as this serves as a warning that all is not well.

Fortunately, nowadays there are many ways in which we can help. With the modern equipment available to us and the various natural and homoeopathic remedies which can be of such help for these conditions, there is little need to suffer endlessly.

In the next chapter I will deal with some related disorders of the cervical vertebrae.

3

Cervical Spondylitis and Spondylosis

Cervical Spondylitis

ALMOST DAILY I hear patients utter remarks like: 'I haven't slept a wink because of this nagging pain in my arm and shoulder', or 'I nearly go out of my mind because of this dreadful ache in my arm', or 'Whatever you consider necessary, please go ahead, so that I may be rid of this stiff and painful arm'.

The above remarks and many more similar complaints I hear about so often fall into the category of illness connected with cervical spondylitis, caused by inflammation of one or more vertebrae. Sometimes this condition can be the cause of long-lasting pains, especially when the attitude is taken that it will go away of its own accord and so nothing is done about it. However, it can also be the cause of very acute pains at the back of the head and in the arms, and even result in loss of feeling in the fingertips. This particular inflammation may be caused by a lesion or even by a draught, and can result in severe discomfort. Professional help is most certainly needed here and the symptoms may be alleviated by sensible treatment of the cause.

26

Heat treatment or massage is frequently used with good results, but my experience is that excellent results for this condition can be obtained by homoeopuncture — a combination of acupuncture and homoeopathy.

Homoeopuncture is a specially designed treatment, which I developed together with my friend, Dr Anton Jayasuriya, while we were both working in the General Hospital in Colombo, Sri Lanka. We used several homoeopathic extracts in combination with the acupuncture needle and the results were most encouraging.

In homoeopuncture, the acupuncture needle is dipped in a homoeopathic extract, the choice of which depends on the patient's complaint. Using the established acupuncture points, the needle is then placed in position, after which electro-stimulation is applied. Some fantastic results have been obtained with this form of treatment, and it has left some rather sceptical patients delighted.

In order to clear inflammation of the joints or discs I use neural therapy and place the dipped needles directly into the inflamed areas. Whereas homoeopuncture is a newly developed and recent finding which brings relief to painful conditions, neural therapy was established many years ago.

Way back in 1925 two doctors, Ferdinand and Walther Huneka, desperately tried to find a cure for their sister's frequently recurring bouts of migraine. During their experiments, they hit upon a drug called Atophanyl. When their sister took this, her headaches would suddenly wane. They stepped up their experiments and discovered that this method also brought surprisingly encouraging results for rheumatic disorders.

Continuing along the same lines they progressed to intravenous and intramuscular injections and discovered the benefits of intramuscular injections of procaine for extremely painful conditions. Of course, this substance would act as a temporary anaesthetic, but the brothers involuntarily hit on certain acupuncture points, which produced similar effects.

Many of the cervical spondylitis, cervical spondylosis or

capsular arthritis patients I treat in my clinic have experienced tremendous benefits from the above treatment methods.

As a result of neural therapy an alteration takes place in the depolarised state of the tissue and, by injecting procaine, an anaesthetic effect is achieved. For many spinal disorders I personally use procaine combined with another natural injection fluid. I also have used this particular combination successfully for painful conditions which are caused by scar tissue.

I remember one particular lady who was suffering severe pains due to a spinal compression in the upper and lower neck area. However, she was terrified of injections, but as her pains were so severe, I was finally able to convince her that the pain would be so much less after treatment and she had little option but to agree to undergo the therapy. The result was a more or less instant relief and it left my patient wondering why she had made such a fuss about an injection.

As this injection is virtually painless, its therapeutic value is invaluable for cervical spondylitis complaints, nerve root compression or spinal cord compression. Although this treatment was discovered way back in 1925, is by no means outmoded and still today surprising results are obtained in its application for spine-related complaints.

Symphosan — one of Dr Vogel's Bioforce remedies — is extremely useful in the treatment of cervical conditions. It shows its versatility in that it may be used internally as well as externally and will reduce swellings or inflamed joints and tendons and connected problems. The main ingredient of Symphosan is *Symphytum officinalis* (comfrey), together with smaller quantities of *Hamamelis virginiana* (witch hazel), *Hypericum* (St John's Wort), *Solidago* (golden rod), *Sanicula europea* (sanicle), *Sempervivum tectorum* (houseleek) and *Arnica montana*.

Another of Dr Vogel's Bioforce remedies is Poho ointment. This I also find of great benefit to sufferers of cervical spondylitis. This remedy is mainly based on St John's Wort, with quantities of peppermint oil, witch-hazel water, calendula, citrus oil and Balsam of Peru. Generally, after just a few applications of Poho ointment, improvement will be clearly noticeable.

It so happened that while I was preparing this particular chapter I received a letter from a Lancastrian lady. I will quote a few lines of this letter as it bears out one of the points I have been trying to make.

Many thanks for all your help, but most of all for your suggestion that I use Symphosan, which indeed has served me better than any drug I have used previously. Would you please be good enough to arrange to have another bottle sent off to me as soon as possible.

Thank you once again for your sound advice.

A further letter I received, from a lady in Kettering, states: 'The treatment has worked beyond belief and the dreadful headaches I used to suffer are now a thing of the past.'

A gentleman from Paisley also wrote to tell me that due to the treatment he had received the unbearable pains he used to suffer in neck, shoulder and arm have now completely vanished. He added that his wife as well is truly grateful because it has meant a total change in their lives. I particularly remember this patient, because he fell into that category I referred to at the start of this chapter, namely those people who live in constant pain, which has come to be a part of their life.

I vividly remember the patient in whom an X-ray showed a very inflamed area near the fifth cervical vertebra. This gave me considerable problems as the lady concerned was physically very weak. She was the wife of a well-known surgeon and did not know where to turn. After careful and gentle manipulation and following the treatment described in the first part of this chapter her pain was fortunately much relieved.

When I had shown her obviously knowledgeable husband the X-ray, he was quite shocked to see the severe inflammation in the area of the fifth cervical vertebra. I had no choice but to use some strong homoeopathic potencies to help ease the pain, among which I selected Radium Bromide 30. Irritation and sensitivity may easily spread to other function and organs which are connected to the spinal cord. If corrective methods are applied, the pain will abate almost immediately. However, if the irritation persists, then other treatment may be necessary.

This case was especially interesting as the lower five cervical vertebrae have typical characteristics. The seventh vertebra, to which the inflammation had spread, adapts the formation of the dorsal vertebrae. As this is the largest of the cervical vertebrae and the spinous process is longest, it is often referred to as the vertebral prominence, as it may be visible or palpably prominent.

I also recall a young lady from a nearby village who came to tell me of her discomfort and that she had been informed she was suffering from a condition called spondylitis, of which she had never heard. She suffered the classical symptoms of dizziness, being unable to walk straight and occasionally suffering lack of feeling in the fingertips.

When I examined her, however, I discovered something unusual. Because I knew her general practitioner quite well, I referred her back to him and discussed the case with him by phone, because my suspicions had been raised. Indeed, not long afterwards, he phoned me with the message that X-rays had shown a massive tumour. An immediate operation had been necessary and because of this action it had been possible to save the patient's life. This goes to show that although these particular complaints are often pushed aside as just another case of spondylitis, it is essential to have it checked out and seen to immediately.

Most cases can be treated without surgery if there is no malignant factor present, but one should always take great care. I remember my first patient one Saturday morning, who asked me to see to his right arm because it was so painful. When we went through his medical history I considered it advisable to take an X-ray before being prepared to make a diagnosis. As our radiographer was due to start about an hour later I discussed this with the patient and asked him to wait for a while.

Unfortunately, my suspicions were confirmed and the X-ray revealed that secondaries were present in his arm. Had I manipulated this patient it would have caused him severe distress and increased his problems further. Again I must stress the necessity of a correct diagnosis, even in what is often considered as a straightforward case.

Mostly, of course, X-ray findings in cervical complaints point to a straightforward inflammation. However, when there is indication of a nerve root disease or spinal cord involvement, a series of X-rays is advisable before deciding on a method of treatment. A single X-ray will not always point the finger at a lesion or a change, due to soft tissue injury, while, nevertheless, dysfunctions are prominent or progressive. Therefore it is essential to delve into the medical background of the patient.

Sometimes patients are advised to wear a surgical collar or undergo traction treatment, but these methods are not always in the best interest of the patient. It might bring some initial relief when a collar is fitted, but one must realise that by doing so the muscles will weaken and if the X-ray confirms that there are no further complications, some gentle manipulation is much more preferable. I am wary of traction, as it would not be the first time that I have seen the problem aggravated as a result. Often some heat and massage treatment will do much more good.

Cervical Spondylosis
This is another cervical muscular condition which can be the reason for pain and distress. This condition is often described as degenerative changes in the intervertebral discs with peripheral ossification, or similarly as osteoarthritis of the spine.

Cervical spondylosis often causes nerve root or spinal

compression pains and can be triggered off by a traumatic experience such as a whiplash. The cause can also be due to osteoarthritis in the neck or, in more simple terms, wear and tear. The latter can produce considerable discomfort, especially if there is a narrowing of the spine or a lipping of intervertebral spaces between the discs, where the nerve roots are under pressure.

These symptoms often rear their heads during middle age or later and frequently result in progressive spastic motor weakness of the lower extremities. The same effects may also be experienced due to old fractures and muscle tension, which can create persistent pains. Cervical spondylosis can also be caused by a herniated disc or by blood diseases.

In a previous book on *Rheumatism, Arthritis and Related Disorders* I have set out several ways in which these conditions can be treated, as well as ways to safeguard or minimise the effects of this or related illnesses.

I remember a very bad case of cervical spondylosis, where even the legs of that particular patient had been affected. I felt very sorry for him as it concerned a busy and energetic businessman and it had caused him considerable problems in his work. He suffered severe bouts of pains in his neck, then his legs would nearly give way under him. His condition had been previously diagnosed as cervical spondylosis, several times over, and as he slowly reacted to the treatment of acupuncture and homoeopuncture, I decided to give him laser treatment as well, which I occasionally use in such cases.

During his very slow progress I remembered a pilot study I was once involved in with patients in Germany who had suffered cervical problems. One of the German professors took the viewpoint that a high dose of vitamin E could be of great benefit to cervical spondylitis or cervical spondylosis patients. This vitamin supplement should go hand in hand with the normal recommended treatment. It was remarkable to see that of the 63 patients who suffered some or other form of cervical condition, a large majority reacted well to a combined vitamin supplement of vitamins E, B1, B6 and B12.

From personal experience, I find that two capsules of vitamin E 400 iu will usually give a great boost in degenerative conditions of this kind. No side-effects have ever been reported and therefore I often advise the following course of treatment for cervical spondylitis or spondylosis patients:

Urticalcin	—a Dr Vogel homoeopathic calcium and silicic acid preparation
Vitamin E	—800 iu daily, or a combination of vitamin E and other vitamins
Imperarthritica	—a Dr Vogel preparation containing:

                                   Polygonum aviculare (Knotgrass)
                                   Solidago virgaurea (Golden Rod)
                                   Petasites officinalis (Butterbur)
                                   Potentilla anserina (Silverweed)
                                   Achillea maschata (Yarrow)
                                   Betula alba a folium (White birch and leaves)
                                   Viscum album (Mistletoe)
                                   Equisetum arvense (Horsetail)
                                   Colchicum autumnale (Meadow saffron)
                                   Mentha pierita (Peppermint)

Sometimes I also add Poho ointment to the above programme. I also generally advise some simple exercises, which can be found in the Appendix of this book.

The case of a promising violin player comes to mind. Although it concerned quite a young girl, there was no doubt that she was subjected to a spondylitic condition and she also displayed arthritic tendencies. She therefore experienced considerable problems when playing the violin. The Principal of the Royal Academy of Music wrote me about his concern for this obviously gifted girl, who was considerably handicapped due to permanent pain. He was worried that she might come to associate pain with her love for music and could see this affecting a promising career.

I made a point of inviting them to one of my seminars in London, where afterwards I took the opportunity to meet her. She told me that she had followed the normal procedures and had visited her general practitioner. X-rays had been made and she had been given osteopathic treatment. Although she had been seen by several specialists, the minute she picked up the violin the pain recurred.

I was intrigued and asked her permission to investigate further. When I examined her spine, I became convinced that I was dealing here with a case of cervical spondylosis. I suggested a change in her diet, as I set great store by correct eating habits and believe that 'we are what we eat', and instructed her accordingly. I also recommended that she use Araniforce, which is a marvellous combination remedy of homoeopathic ingredients, and I taught her some exercises. Straightaway, that evening, I gave her some gentle manipulation and asked her to visit me at my clinic in Scotland, where I could give her further treatment.

I was delighted when later her principal wrote to me again with the message that the girl had asked him to inform me she was feeling so much better and she was now able to sleep better, because for the first time in twelve years she was not plagued by pains. He added that the encouragement I had been able to give her was bound to be beneficial to her career and once again stressed his pupil's gratitude.

I am aware of the fact that alternative medicine is often looked upon with scepticism, but let us not forget that it provides us with many safe methods, which are often invaluable for these problems.

A letter from another patient states his gratitude for his treatment, which resulted in him feeling on top of the world for the first time in five years, as he was totally free from pain in his neck and shoulder. He continued to explain that he had already arranged his next appointment, which he fully intended to keep, in order to find out what he could do to safeguard and maintain this improvement.

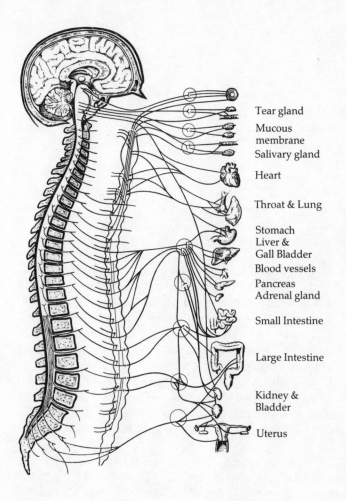

Tear gland

Mucous
membrane

Salivary gland

Heart

Throat & Lung

Stomach
Liver &
Gall Bladder

Blood vessels

Pancreas
Adrenal gland

Small Intestine

Large Intestine

Kidney &
Bladder

Uterus

4

Cranial Osteopathy

WHEN I CONSIDER cranial osteopathy as a section of osteopathy as a whole, I cannot fail to mention the late Denis Brookes, my teacher and one of the most capable and admirable practitioners in this field. He was a well-trained practitioner and an excellent cranial specialist, who has been able to not only help many people in his ever busy practice, but also to make himself available for lectures and training seminars.

Among his patients Denis Brookes counted people who suffered from menstrual problems, asthma, headaches and migraines, as well as treating children. I have seen him use and develop techniques in these cases which he himself had learned in America.

I remember learning, listening to his seminars, that these techniques were even effective for people with eyesight problems and diabetes. Traumatic injuries were treated by relatively simple manipulation and, along with the marvellous training he arranged, he also instilled his motto in his students, which I still often repeat in my own practice: 'Find it, fix it and leave it!'

Whatever and wherever the problem may be, in the spine or in other parts of the human body, any well-trained practitioner should follow this path of finding the cause, fixing the trouble and then leaving the problem area untouched.

It is no use for a practitioner, if he is in any doubt, to 'have a go'. He must be certain of his diagnosis and techniques and the years' experience will render the practitioner more skilled in tracing and adjusting disorders. Cranial osteopathy falls into the category in which a thorough knowledge is essential alongside osteopathic skills. Only then will the afflicted person be able to benefit. Little or insufficient knowledge of the subject can cause more harm than good.

The reader may wonder what cranial osteopathy actually is. To put it in a nutshell it basically comes down to a thorough working knowledge of the inter-relationship between the bone system and the cranium. Both these parts contain not only nerves and brain tissue, but also fibrous material.

It is generally believed that the skull consists only of a bony structure, but nothing is further from the truth. The bones of the skull change and are alive, as they move in a harmonious fashion throughout our lifespan. The strong, fibrous tissue connections with the spinal cord and the sacrum, which reach even as far as the coccyx, are of great importance and the circulatory function should be working harmoniously. The blood and the cerebrospinal fluid work through different channels of the brain and the central nervous system. The cerebrospinal fluid carries hormonal secretions which ensure that the whole circulatory mechanism, if normal, will work effectively.

A good cranial osteopath should be able to discover where the harmony is disturbed with a simple touch. Often, mobility may be restored by simple palpation or pressure. The less force used the better and the patient will generally be immediately aware of the results, and experience an alleviation of the pain.

Ron McCarthy is a good friend and colleague of mine who was also trained by Denis Brookes and whose work I admire greatly. When we were recently lecturing in Malaga, Spain, I was plagued by a headache, possibly because of the very heavy programme which was set out for us there. Within seconds, Ron McCarthy was able to rid me of this headache by simply placing his fingers on a specific area of the skull. Thanks to this action my energy was recharged, so that I felt able to tackle another lecture that evening.

This is one of the reasons why cranial osteopathy is so very suitable for people with vertigo, tinnitis or Ménière's disease. It is also an excellent treatment for facial neuralgia and it often happens with, for example, a distortion of the jawbone, that one particular adjustment of the jaw in relation to the cranium brings immediate relief to those who suffer. My great friend, Dr Wilhelm Khoe from America, has taught me that with one particular adjustment and slight pressure to the skull, it is even possible to cure people of sciatica.

After all these years, it still occasionally surprises me how vitally important harmony in the body is, and how the slightest disharmony throws the correct functioning out of balance. It is indeed like the proverbial pebble which is thrown into the water. The pebble will sink immediately out of sight, but the ripples caused on the water are comparable to the effects of a disharmony in the body, where the causative factor may be difficult to trace, but the symptoms are there for all to see. This is why the words of Denis Brookes are so correct: 'Find it, fix it and leave it!'

Among other disorders which may be adjusted by cranial osteopathic treatment may be included allergic and menstrual problems or hormonal imbalances. Very important also is the treatment by cranial osteopathy of children and even babies.

Especially in newly-born babies, we will see that in an underdeveloped cerebrospinal system, which is still immature in the cranium, the cartilaginous membranes are easily damaged. This can lead to problems in later life. The slightest disorder at this young age may be corrected quickly by an experienced cranial osteopath applying some gentle pressure in the correct place, thus saving the child from likely misery in later life.

I remember a young child, aged three years, who suffered from a mild form of cerebral palsy. When the mother brought the child to me, I almost immediately realised that the problem had arisen at birth. Without her even realising it, I very gently managed to correct the disorder. Despite its age the child was already on a course of drug treatment and I advised the mother to administer Loranthus from Dr Vogel, which is an extract of the mistletoe which grows in the wild oak. With Loranthus in combination with vitamin B12, it was possible to wean this young child from the previously prescribed drugs and the toddler's health problems were greatly improved.

A young Asian boy had virtually no movement in his left arm due to spastic paralysis. After some gentle palpation of the skull and some homoeopathic remedies, amongst which I included Loranthus, this child now has almost full movement of his arm. If it can be discovered what has caused the disharmony, corrective treatment can be administered which will often result in an improved condition.

We are well aware of the fact that the head and neck are of extreme importance. Therefore the development and application of cranial osteopathy is essential in order to help those whose lives are affected due to cranial distortions. Andrew T. Still, the founder of osteopathy, said in a few well-chosen words: 'An osteopath must find the true corners as set by the divine surveyor.'

Very often with the particular technique of cranial osteopathy, we discover entrapments in the fluid flow which isolate the flow in the fluid systems in several ways. Perhaps these are considered of minor importance, yet these functions deserve our full attention. If a correction of a possibly severe lesion is necessary, extreme care is essential and the corrective treatment may stretch to quite a few treatment sessions in order to gently and gradually normalise the functions of the cerebrospinal fluid.

I remember the case of a patient with paralysis, due to

pressure in the lateral side of the skull. With the aid of some other techniques, I discovered that the causative factor was a polyneuralgia. Guided by X-rays, we managed to help this patient and the therapy included some homoeopathic remedies as well as laser treatment. The clearly noticeable improvement certainly made every effort worthwhile.

From personal experience in my practice I believe that a lesion of the occipital mastoid creates an inter-relation with the coccyx. With the present development of laser techniques I reckon that any manipulation to the occiput and the coccyx stimulates the transmission of messages to the central nervous system to influence the occipital mastoid. If there is a lession that is where the cause of the problem will be and by working on both the occiput and the coccyx, relief will be accomplished. The relaxation in the patient will then almost be tangible. In some of the really severe spinal cases I have treated, acupuncture treatment combined with laser treatment brought the sought-after results.

When looking at all the different techniques one has to understand the various essential functions of the coccyx:

—the existent mobility of the central nervous system;
—the mobility of the cranial bones;
—the mobility of the sacrum;
—the tension in the membranes;
—the mobility of the cerebrospinal fluid.

With sensitive touch and gentle palpation one can discover the direction of the forces quite clearly and a cranial mechanism dysfunction will soon be detected by the hands of a skilled practitioner. A good check of the lymphatics will quickly show whether there is any distortion in the respiratory circulatory functions. The cerebrospinal fluid movement will be affected by any problems in this field.

As I have mentioned before, the cranium and the sacrum move as one unit during inspiration and expiration. With close scrutiny, an increase and decrease of the lumbar curvature can be observed during inspiration and expiration.

I once read that the brain seems to rest on a water bed of cerebrofluid and is very active in the arterial, venous and lymphatic flows. A thorough check of the lymphatic system will show if there is lymphatic congestion. In cases of congestion the correct cranial technique is to apply certain pressure in order to normalise the position of the cranial bones. This can be influenced, slowly and gradually, by good relaxation, which may be achieved with the help of some simple breathing exercises which the patient should be taught by the practitioner.

If there is any congestion of the breathing I recommend the use of a natural remedy from Dr Vogel's Bioforce range, called Echinaforce. This acts as a natural antibiotic.

Cranial disorders relate themselves, without any doubt, to every function of the body alignment. Any cranial distortion requires careful observation of the entire cranium, ie both frontal and occipital areas. Sometimes it is even noticeable from the position of the ears if there is an imbalance which needs to be looked at. It could be an indication of disharmony if one ear is placed higher than the other. The forehead might show a bulge, or one eye might be slightly larger than the other. These may all be signs of some trauma, but thanks to the modern techniques now available to us, these irregularities may often be corrected quickly.

Movement, as well as inspiration and expiration, should work quite freely and when working in these sensitive fields, a gentle touch is required. Imagining what happens inside will aid the practitioner to work on the outside.

A careful consideration of all these factors will prove that no indication should be overlooked or ignored. Never should any forceful manipulative techniques, especially on the head or on the neck, be applied. When there is disharmony in the patient's rhythm, it is usually possible to relieve pains or distress with a simple touch.

5

The Dorsal Spine

THE DORSAL or thoracic spine is comprised of twelve vertebrae and is the longest section of the spinal cord. If we study the diagrams in this book we realise how many vital functions it performs. Looking at the anatomical part of the dorsal spine, it becomes clear that some problems actually stem from conditions which prevailed at a young age.

Lordosis, which is a curvature of the spinal column in both the dorsal and the cervical section, can quite frequently be blamed on poor posture. It can also have originated in babyhood. The conventional pram is certainly much more suitable for correct posture for the baby than the popular modern 'buggy', where the baby's spine is curved while it rests. A baby's spinal column is still developing and the bones are not fully calcified. Short trips to the shops with the baby in a buggy are unlikely to cause any permanent damage, but if the baby were to be kept regularly for longer stretches of time in a buggy, spinal abnormalities could well result.

A curvature of the spine can, then, result in a lordosis, which is a convexity forwards and an exaggeration of a normal curve towards the lumbar part of the spine. This is often referred to as a 'hollow back'. On the other hand a 'kyphosis' may develop, which is a backwards convexity, usually present in the dorsal region, and faulty posture can exacerbate this problem. This is mostly seen in tall, slim people and can usually be corrected by good exercises.

An older term for kyphosis is a 'humpback', which describes an angular deformity of the spine. Again the advice is that a strict exercise programme be adhered to and in osteopathy we often have to remind our patients that the bones do not move, but that the muscles actually move the bones. Therefore, the more work that is done on the muscular system the better. People with humpbacks or round backs are able to counteract their deformities to a certain extent if attention is paid to a good exercise programme.

Another form of lateral curvature of the spine is referred to as scoliosis. This condition often reveals itself in that the patient's spine seems to be shaped like a question mark. This is sometimes caused by a disc lesion to one side of the spinal cord and muscular spasms can be experienced. We do know that scoliosis can be of a permanent nature if nothing is done about it and again I stress the necessity that immediate attention is paid to spinal problems and that expert advice in relation to these conditions is sought *and* heeded. Physical exercise and acupuncture treatment is beneficial, as well as correct dietary management to strengthen the vertebrae.

A vertebra consists of two parts:

—the front, sometimes called the anterior;
—the rear, also called the posterior.

The anterior and posterior arches enclose the spinal cord and form a strong pillar for the support of the total spine, spinal nerves and blood vessels. These are protected by the nucleus pulposus, which is a gelatinous substance. In this respect the protecting jelly, as I often call it, should be made as strong as possible and for this reason I maintain that good

43

dietary management is essential. I also advise the use of Symphosan, Comfrey or Urticalcin, which often prove to be of great help.

Where movement seems to be restricted, we mostly find that this originates from the upper dorsal area, namely dorsal 1 or dorsal 2. However, when problems arise on dorsal 7 or 8, it can have more serious repercussions. Just such a case comes to mind while writing this and it creates sad memories, as it concerned one of my dearest friends, whom I have since lost.

Her case is an excellent example to quote here when pointing out that any suspected spinal condition does warrant full and careful consideration. I was shocked when, after her funeral abroad, I learned about the cause of her death.

It concerned a hard-working and very knowledgeable Dutch lady of around the age of forty. She lost her life as a result of what was thought to have been a minor traffic accident. She had set out on her bicycle to run an errand. Unfortunately, a car hit the rear of her bike and she was thrown over the handlebars. She was taken to hospital with what seemed a mild concussion and X-rays were made of the head and the neck area. No X-rays of the dorsal area appeared necessary, as there seemed to be no problem there. It was thought that one or two days in hospital would see her back on her feet.

However, her condition did not improve and she suddenly appeared to suffer breathlessness and felt uncomfortable. When her husband arrived at the appointed visiting hour he was told that the specialist wanted to speak to him. He was subsequently informed that his wife had died after experiencing sudden breathing difficulties.

My friend had always been slightly asthmatic, and what had actually happened was that pressure had built up on the 7th and 8th dorsal vertebrae. This resulted in additional pressure on the 9th dorsal vertebra, which put her heart under strain. Any pressure like this can be the cause of a heart attack, which in her case proved fatal. Her heart had not been able to cope with the pressure and she unfortunately died.

A clear indication of this intricate area can be seen in the diagrams in this book. Even if an X-ray had been made of the whole spine, it is still unlikely that any irregularities in this particular section would have been revealed. The sensitive fingers of a qualified osteopath, though, would have detected unusual pressure and by simple palpation could have relieved this pressure, and I feel that my dear friend's life could perhaps have been saved.

It happens every now and then that when remedial work on the dorsal area has taken place, for example when a condition commonly referred to as a slipped disc has been treated, the patient will afterwards inform me that his or her constipation problem has suddenly and unaccountably disappeared. They rarely realise that this can be quite easily explained because manipulation of the lower dorsal area will have a general loosening effect in that region.

Another example of side-benefits is that manipulation of the 3rd, 4th or 5th dorsal vertebrae can bring relief to asthmatic people. This is borne out by a letter I received from a young girl who had always had to rely on inhalers and sprays for her asthmatic condition. After a series of manipulative treatment sessions of the spine, she experienced a totally unexpected relief in her breathing. I also advised her to do some simple breathing exercises and in this way she could look forward to a life which was virtually clear of asthmatic attacks. In a letter addressed to me she wrote:

> I remember the time that my mother phoned you because I was struggling so much with my breathing. You advised her to place an ice-pack on a specific area of my spine and this instantly eased my condition. As you know, now my breathing has improved so immensely that I want to thank you from the bottom of my heart.

Such letters serve to encourage me in the work I am doing in order to try and help as many people as possible. In our work, however, we should never forget that no matter how much satisfaction we get from bringing about relief of pain, it should always remain our main ambition to locate the cause of the problem and set about rectifying this.

The distribution of energy is very important to the spine. We know that the life force which runs through the body, and which motivates all the organs, is indeed a force to be reckoned with. This life force operates in the physical body as well as in the mental body and deserves to be guided and transported to the best of our ability.

Energy imbalance in relation to back problems very often accumulates according to emotional conditions. When the energy supply to the back muscles is less than efficient, vertebrae may be pulled out of position by imbalanced muscles. Occasionally, instead of using manipulation on the misplaced vertebrae, if it is possible to influence the energy supply to the spinal muscles, the vertebrae may again balance themselves spontaneously.

The body has a great capacity for innate healing and possesses a restoring power which can work quickly and effectively. Therefore the practitioner should be trained in all there is to know about the energy distribution of the spine. With any chronic back problems remedial methods may be used and whenever digestion, kidney functioning or breathing improves, we know that we are on the right road to recovery.

Very often the question is put to me as to what kind of energy is most useful. This is a very difficult question to answer because we are still learning about the various possibilities available to us in the field of energy, as so many forms of energy exist and so much more research is needed.

What we do know, however, is that the life force within the body may be influenced negatively as well as positively, and with the help of magnetic therapy, negative and positive forces may be balanced very effectively.

Once I was visited by Dr Bodgener from America, who wrote the excellent book *The Unbalanced Magnetic Field and Health Integration*. The minute he stepped into my surgery, it amazed me that with the very first patient we saw, he immediately spotted an imbalance in the spinal cord. He stated that this patient had some quite serious kidney problems. I was aware of these, but he had not seen this person's medical record before coming to this diagnosis. By using his magnetic instruments he had come to this conclusion and I was grateful that he was willing to teach me some of his methods.

Years ago, I saw a famous American chiropractor at work. Dr Gonstead was an authority on disc functioning. He found that in cases of disc malfunction, ligaments of the joints which had lost their integrative proprioceptive connection with the central nervous system, could be wedged onto this related spinal process. The joint, including the disc, could be wedged to the left or the right and very often pain was the result.

Dr Gonstead demonstrated how, by gentle touch, correction of this problem could be achieved. The wedged disc cannot adequately act as a solid central area of stabilisation on which peripheral movement is made possible. The technique used by Dr Gonstead is aimed at restoring disc integrity and, to this degree, the disc adjustment tends to restore the total integration.

Dr Cunningham describes the intervertebral disc as the undercarriage of our body, which is united to the upper-carriage of the body by means of a fibro-cartilaginous intervertebral disc. The annulus fibrosis — the protecting jelly area — is the peripheral part and is composed of fibro-cartilage. These fibres run between two vertebrae and are arranged in rings. The centre consists of the nucleus pulposus — a soft and elastic composition of a pulpy fibrous material containing cells. Functionally this serves as a cushion between vertebrae and its elastic properties ensure that there is always a small range of motion.

In the dorsal spine a small proportion of fibro-cartilage, relative to the length of the thoracic region, is necessary for its anterior posterior movement. The intervertebral disc, which is like a part structure, is found between the bodies of the vertebrae from inferior articulation of the axis to and including the lumbo-sacral joint.

The intervertebral disc consists of layers of fibro-cartilage and fibrous tissue, arranged in a circular fashion around a central space. In each successive layer the fibres are directed alternately in an oblique superior and inferior fashion, between the upper and lower surface of the adjoining vertebral bodies. The fibrous rings of the discs are grossly termed the annulus fibrosis, while the spongy fibro-cartilage contained within the rings is called the annulus spongiosa.

Near the centre of the disc the laminations become progressively less distinct, and are absent in the central core. The central area, comprising about one quarter of the vertebral body is filled with a fine gelatinous substance known as the nucleus pulposus. The thickness of the disc varies, being greatest in the lumbar region where it is about one-third the thickness of the vertebral body. Then the discs become successively thinner in the higher level, being smallest in the cervical spine, where they comprise about one-sixth the thickness of the vertebral body. The thickness of the disc is greatest at its central core.

I maintain that being aware of these facts encourages us to take more care of our dietary management. It is a fact that a correct diet, together with palpation or magnetic therapy, using neuro-dynamic techniques, or sometimes laser treatment, often makes forceful manipulation redundant.

Many techniques have been designed which may serve as self-help methods and it would be sensible to indulge in these, because there is a lot of truth in the old saying: 'You are as old as your spine'. Keep active with swimming, cycling, walking or with some of the special exercises which I will describe in detail in the Appendix of this book.

If we do consider applying pressure techniques to the dorsal area, we should realise that a little palpation, done with the thumbs only, on certain areas can easily be done at home. This method was especially designed by my great friend Dr Leonard J. Allan. The specific spinal areas and the symptoms to look for, before applying this simple technique, are listed in the schedule at the end of this chapter. Very slight pressure on these areas will help to release a lot of the existing tension.

I remember a young lady who regularly suffered from severe headaches, averaging about three times a week. She had been to see several doctors who had not been able to diagnose any cause for her problems. She had also informed them that she frequently suffered from bouts of dizziness, as well as nausea, but they had not been able to find anything wrong with her. The X-rays I had ordered showed, however, that there was a slight wedging between the 4th and 5th dorsal vertebrae and a little distortion. After a few gentle pressure treatments to this particular area, the distortion balanced itself and regained a normal pattern.

There was a middle-aged gentleman with dorsal problems and some pain in his lower back. His sacrum had tilted to the right with a very slight wedging of the 6th and 7th dorsal. He was quite weak and could not take any manipulation at all. After balancing his spine with acupuncture, the nerve reflexes and corresponding muscles improved considerably. He then was able to endure some palpation on the area where he suffered the worst pain and after three treatments he was delighted about how the pains had diminished. I maintained steady pressure on his most painful area, which reduced the pain, then I palpated the occipital area and after that the coccyx area. After this treatment he experienced a distinct change in his whole condition.

With thumbs only, I went on to very gently adjust the spinal area and I checked the weak muscles, after which the little adjustment seemed to become stronger. We must understand that if there is any subluxation, as was slightly present in this patient, we cannot separate its relationship from the entire body, so an evaluation of the total condition is necessary.

In front of me I have a letter from a lady who was in severe pain along the whole dorsal spine area, due to a subluxation which had never been properly seen to. She writes:

> I want to thank you most sincerely for the relief which I now experience from the pains that have haunted me for 33 years.

> I have informed my doctor about the successful outcome of the three treatments I have had from you and I am sure that he will be equally delighted.

I did indeed receive a letter from the doctor also, in which he thanked me for the relief his patient had gained after such a long and painful struggle.

Another letter I will quote is from a patient who was in severe discomfort and whose stomach and constipation problems were greatly eased after treatment. She wrote:

> As Christmas approaches I think back to the way I felt one year ago and I can't decide on the right words to express my gratitude for the change in my health. I work, as I did then, but the difference is that hard work is now so easy and such fun. I feel that life is again wonderful, for which I thank you.

The question remains of why, nowadays, there are so many spinal problems about. We must of course realise that in our modern lifestyle our bodies are often abused and/or pampered:

—we generally take insufficient exercise;
—we tend to sleep in beds which are far too soft;
—we spend long hours behind the wheel of a car;
—we relax by curling up in soft and cosy chairs.

There are so many ways in which we abuse our bodies and place unnecessary added stress on them. The accumulative effect is often neck and back pains.

Chronic strain should therefore not be neglected and if we look at our lifestyle, most of us will be able to adapt, in some way or another, in order to minimise or at least reduce the outcome of some of the excessive demands we place on our bodies.

Dr Leonard J. Allan's Schedule
The spinal areas and symptoms to look for before applying the

neuro-dynamic technique are detailed below. The spinal processes are usually tender on palpation.

Dorsal 1:   The heart — insufficient circulation — food and waste carry off occurring in the heart

Dorsal 2:   Heart valve and nerve control involvement

Dorsal 3:   Diaphragm, pleura or lung involvement

Dorsal 4:   Common bile duct — highly strung, nervous individual; may be developing liver, pancreatic or digestive disorders

Dorsal 5:   (a) Stomach involvement
              (b) If D.3 and D.5 are found to be tender, you can expect a hiatus hernia

Dorsal 6:   (a) Pancreas not working properly
              (b) The Islets of Langerhans out of control

Dorsal 7:   Lymphatic involvement — spleen processes abnormal, foreign toxic substance

Dorsal 8:   Liver involvement — toxins in small intestines — inability to get rid of them

Dorsal 9:   Adrenal gland misfunction

Dorsal 10:   Small intestines involved — inability to emulsify fats from lack of bile; this ruins the muscosa, will soon lose ability to eat like a horse

Dorsals 11 and 12:   Kidney function abnormal

51

6

Cervical and Dorsal Spinal Complaints

THERE ARE NUMEROUS complaints relating to the cervical and dorsal spine. I intend to deal with some of the most common ones in this chapter, at the same time adding some practical advice in the form of hints as to what may be done at home to ease the situation and what methods are available to the practitioner.

Let us consider, however, the fact that, as mentioned before, many problems result from stressful situations, which cause muscle contractions which in turn produce dis-alignments in the cervical and dorsal spine. For example, a typist sitting in the wrong position will cause tension on one particular part of the neck and shoulders, thereby exaggerating the situation. Most certainly this is not the only job which is conducive to spinal problems. Those people in jobs which are likely to put strain on the spine are especially advised to exercise in their free time. The last chapter of this book contains a range of special exercises which enable people to relieve some of the tension which builds up daily.

Headaches, or 'dizzy heads', as they are often called, are

also often the result of incorrect posture. I would agree that some people are more prone to tension in their everyday life because of work-related problems, but this tension can be alleviated by gentle manipulation.

The reactions to this tension can vary greatly from one person to the next. It can present itself as a frozen shoulder, a tennis elbow or a golf elbow, a football knee or a housemaid's knee.

These problems are very relevant today, because the human movement pattern has changed so much over the last few decades. We tend to lead a much more sedentary life, due to a variety of reasons, such as private motorised transport, labour-saving gadgets in the home, mechanisation of industry and agriculture and longer holidays. These last are mostly used to relax, which is the whole purpose of holidays, but much time is spent just lounging about. There is in fact a whole list of causes, which for obvious reasons I will not extend further here.

It is, however, a realistic statement that our legs have become extended acceleration pedals. It should then not surprise us that spinal disorders have become more common. Good control over the joints, the muscles and especially the spine is very much a case of proper and sufficient exercise.

Let us deal with some of the previously mentioned disorders one by one. I will start with golf and tennis elbows, which are not infrequent nowadays.

Golf and Tennis Elbows
What really are they? The most common of the two is the tennis elbow. It is experienced as a severe pain, felt over the outer aspect at the top of the elbow; a pain which arises from excessive lifting, gripping or twisting movements, and which causes weakness and restriction of movement.

The cause of a tennis elbow can be cervical disalignment or a lesion. Some people have suffered on and off from this condition over a long period of time. The hundreds of people with tennis elbows I have treated over the years, though, have mostly been cured by manipulation. Added to this, a neural therapy injection right into the tender and soft tissue nearly always brings relief.

From experience I would say that if the area is severely inflamed, the quickest results are obtained if we use either Diapulse, laser or ultra-sound treatment.

There have obviously been cases which have not shown any favourable reaction to any of the above mentioned therapies, but strangely enough those cases have responded well to gentle magnetic treatment.

However, sometimes I suspect that tennis elbows and golf elbows are not caused by structural complaints, but may be due to a deficiency. I remember when at one time I was joined in my clinic by Dr Hans Moolenburgh from the Netherlands. He lent a hand and dealt with quite a few patients, but afterwards told me that he was amazed by the number of golf and tennis elbows he had come across during the few days he had been working with me. I have now come to believe that as the soil in Scotland is especially deficient in zinc, some of these complaints may be eradicated if patients are given an additional quantity of this mineral. In some particularly chronic cases I have tested this theory and must admit that I was delighted with the results.

In research we applied this theory to the magnetic therapy and found that zinc not only has a tremendous healing influence on wounds, but also in these types of case. In severe cases which had failed to respond to cortisone injections given by the patients' doctors we have tried a combination of zinc and vitamin E with surprisingly good results.

How badly a tennis elbow can affect us can be realised from a letter I received from a young man who was totally handicapped due to this problem. He had been told by his doctor that he had to rest his arm completely, and indeed had done so for quite a while without any benefit whatsoever. The alternative treatment prescribed by his practitioner was an operation, and so he decided to come and see me before agreeing to such a dramatic decision. Fortunately, I was able to help him and the problem was completely solved. In his letter he wrote that life was now so much more pleasurable since he was now free of this ever-stinging pain.

Living in that part of the country where golf has strong roots and where several championship golf courses are positioned, I have been asked for treatment by many golfers, amateurs as well as professionals. Among these have indeed been some very famous ones, with problems encountered in the run-up to the Open tournament, which is held in this area at frequent intervals. With very simple corrective movements I have been able to ease their pain so that they could continue to play in the championships. Needless to say, it is not only during the Open tournaments that I am called on to treat golf elbows as I count many golfers as well as other sportsmen among my patients.

Severe cases of golf and tennis elbows are greatly helped by an injection into the area of the epicondyles, as prescribed in the neural therapy.

Tennis elbows tend to be more common than golf eblows, but they can be equally painful. Neither bears any particular relationship to the sport they are named after. For a layman it is very difficult to differentiate between the two.

Bursitis
Another condition which I include in this category is bursitis, which is either an acute or chronic inflammation of a bursa — a sac or a cavity containing a fluid that reduces friction. Bursae are found where tendons pass by bony areas. The deep bursae communicate with the joints. Bursitis mostly occurs in the shoulder, but other fairly common forms of this affliction are the miner's elbow, the housemaid's knee and, sometimes, the first metatarsal head bunions.

Although it is said that no source is known for bursitis, it is frequently thought to be caused by traumatic experiences, inflammation or infection. The pain with bursitis can be really quite drastic and although localised, it can affect a large area. Sometimes a swelling will appear, or redness accompanied by pain, and thereafter muscle weakness and limitation of movement will often be experienced. From the X-rays we often see the presence of calcifications and it is these calcifications that are the major source of the pain. This can be so severe that I have seen patients faint because of even one single movement.

The best results for bursitis I have obtained have been with acupuncture treatment, laser therapy and very gentle manipulation. To aid these therapies I also recommend the use of the Bioforce remedy Imperarthritica, and the massaging in of Symphosan and Poho ointment, alternately. The patient undergoing this treatment is usually delighted with the relief obtained from it. Gentle exercises are recommended and hot packs of olive-oil or castor-oil will help to ease the pain.

I remember a young girl whose case history I looked at again the other day. She had suffered from bursitis for a long time and had been advised to have an operation. Her employer was a veterinary surgeon and he suggested that she made an appointment to see me before deciding in favour of an operation. After successful treatment she wrote:

> Just a note to let you know how delighted I was today after the third treatment. I am again able to use a tin opener properly for the first time in eight months. As you can see from my handwriting, I am also able to write again. Admittedly it goes slowly, and maybe it is not as neat as my usual handwriting, but it is great to know that at least I can WRITE again.

Tendinitis and Tenosynovitis
Both of these conditions are caused by inflammation of the lining of the sheaths of the tendons. The synovial-lined tendon sheath is usually the site of the inflammation, which often results from a calcium deposit. As I have already said in relation to some of the disorders dealt with previously, no one is totally sure about the cause, but it seems certain that this condition is mostly aggravated by trauma, strain or drastic exercises.

Tendinitis and Tenosynovitis can affect the shoulder capsule and associated tendons, the hamstrings or the Achilles tendons. I have often treated footballers, athletes and other sportsmen for these conditions. However, these injuries are not always sports-related.

Once an operation has been performed to ease this condition, treatment becomes much more difficult. Where an operation has not been successful, the condition is often actually worse than before. Those patients who have undergone an unsuccessful operation should take Oil of Evening Primrose capsules, which usually help the post-trauma effects. Either acupuncture or laser treatment can also bring relief.

If these conditions are treated in their early stages, or when acute, we can usually prevent the follow-on chronic conditions, which I will discuss next.

Frozen Shoulder
A frozen shoulder is a general term used to describe pain and limitation of movement in the joint and can be due to a variety of causes. Thinking of those people who go through the trauma of a frozen shoulder and considering the suffering involved, one cannot be careful enough in trying to prevent such a condition. The frozen shoulder will react well to magnetic treatment, acupuncture or ultra-sound, as do the previously listed disorders.

In the main, though, I treat frozen shoulders with homoeopuncture, ie acupuncture with a needle which has been dipped in a homoeopathic substance. This is generally followed up by laser treatment and the recommended use of Symphosan and Poho ointment. This programme is completed by gentle exercises on which the patient will be instructed.

I suggest that a rolled-up towel is placed under the armpits and then the arms should be gently pressed into the body. If this is done regularly and systematically, these patients will regain a greater degree of movement, and consequently relief.

I know that any patient who has a frozen shoulder will do whatever is necessary to ease the situation as this condition can linger on seemingly endlessly. Professional help from an osteopathic practitioner increases the chances of pain relief drastically.

I am often asked by concerned patients where the trouble stemmed from in the first place and why it should be so painful. We must realise that any pain in these regions is due to the important task that the head, neck and shoulders and all our upper limbs for that matter, are supposed to perform. In order to function correctly a high level of mobility is required and the neck and shoulders carry a lot of weight. Forceful exercise, a wrong movement or even draughty conditions can cause an inflammation of a joint, ligament, muscle or nerve and result in stress. Pain radiation may affect the nerve root resulting in sensitivity and pain.

Osteopathy, which in effect is a complete health caring programme, has been especially successful over the many years of its existence in these above-mentioned conditions.

I like to recall the saying of Dr C. B. Atzen:

> Osteopathy is the name of that system of the healing art, which places chief emphasis on the structural integrity of the body mechanism as being the most important single factor in the maintenance of the well-being of the organism in health or disease.

Another saying, this time from the very able osteopathic practitioner C. H. Downing, goes:

> Osteopathy is a philosophy of medicine. Healing signifies a complete system of therapeutics basing its treatment of all abnormal conditions of the body on the natural laws and vital principles governing life, namely the adjustment of all these vital forces of the body, whether physical, chemical or mental, in so far as we have knowledge thereof.

The above explains my reasons for advocating that

alternative medicine should go hand-in-hand with orthodox medicine, as each system has its advantages and the patients would reap the benefits from such co-operation.

I see this expressed in a testimonial from a patient who said that his wife had found such considerable relief from the treatment she had received for her very badly damaged shoulder and upper arm. The whole family was delighted and grateful for the treatment, which was given as a supplement to the traditional physiotherapy treatment, prescribed by her hospital practitioner. Her physiotherapist was also completely happy with the way both treatments inter-related. This particular patient had been involved in a traffic accident and had suffered badly. However, thanks to the treatment she now felt so much better.

A letter from another patient with a prolonged frozen shoulder condition reads: 'The acupuncture treatment has helped so well that now, for the first time in months, I am free of pain. Hopefully this will mean the end of this persistent painful condition and I want you to accept my heartfelt thanks for your efforts and the encouraging results.'

Just how penetrating these disorders of the cervical and dorsal spine can be, and their effect on other parts of the body, became clear when I treated an elderly patient who came all the way from Middlesex to my clinic in Scotland. A relative had offered to drive her north because of the more or less constant tingling in the fingers. She had become virtually incapacitated. Some time after I had treated her, I received a letter which stated: 'I like this new-found feeling of well-being. I have now got full movement back in my fingers, hands and shoulders and how good it is to feel what I consider "normal" again.'

There are of course a whole range of disorders and complaints where osteopathy will be of help. This will be confirmed by many of my arthritic patients, in whom localised joints had shown signs of degeneration. Here again careful osteopathic treatment proves its value. In my previous book about arthritic and rheumatic disorders I have mentioned many of the therapies available. That book also contains some simple home treatments, which the patient is free to adopt into their individual lifestyle.

With a little adjustment of the upper dorsal spine and manipulation of the fifth dorsal vertebra, many people have found a reduction in not only their breathing and/or asthmatic problems, but also in chest pains and functional heart distress.

I remember an asthmatic patient who suffered bad bouts of breathing difficulties. After a simple adjustment of the fifth dorsal vertebra the improvement was near enough immediate. Not only asthmatic complaints and bronchitis are served well by spinal manipulation, but also where chronic or acute obstruction is present, the respiratory function of the patient will improve. The obstructing mucus will be loosened, so that it can be cleared and a better breathing pattern may be established.

Digestive complaints often benefit as well when an improved balance is found in the working of the spine and here too manipulative adjustment of the ninth dorsal vertebra can bring about a pleasing change.

A nice testimonial I received from a grateful patient goes as follows: 'However is it possible that after years of pill-swallowing my migraine headaches have disappeared. Totally unexpectedly, though, the menstrual problems I have been plagued with for so long also seem to have ceased to bother me.' As I have already mentioned, even these conditions can be alleviated by spinal adjustment.

I should not forget to mention here that infuriating problem called tinnitus, which exasperates its sufferers and, to quote some, 'makes their lives hell'. Its symptoms are frequent, if not constant, ringing, hissing and buzzing in the ears. One of my patients was so badly affected that she constantly walked around with a 'walkman' on her head in an effort to drown out the sounds in her head. With manipulation, acupuncture treatment and some laser treatment we managed to clear up this problem for her, to her extreme delight.

Each of the above-mentioned conditions can be such a

limitation to individuals and once their problem has been sorted, their outlook on life often changes drastically.

Mechanical and personal factors may play a part in these undesirable conditions. Poor posture, or anything that will affect the structural integrity of the spinal column, will have repercussions and will also affect other organs, eg the important endocrine glands. Small lesions in the cervical and in the thoracic spinal area will also affect the brain. Hence my reasoning that any spinal conditions deserve careful attention.

I remember a lady who had travelled from abroad specifically to attend our clinic because, as she claimed, she was slowly being driven mad by the pain. I discovered that apart from a really severe problem in her neck and dorsal spine, she was also affected by the carpal tunnel syndrome. As she had done quite a lot of reading on the subject of the spinal structure as a whole, I tried to explain the situation to her. Having discovered some lesions in her hand and wrist, we pointed out to her that it was worth remembering that there is an inter-communicating articular cavity of the joints to the dorsal convexity of the hand. The arch formed by the wedge-shaped heads of the carpal bones had narrowed. Only by treating all these joints and lesions, could she expect any improvement. Indeed, we were able to treat her successfully and, although she had to undergo prolonged treatment, she ultimately regained a normal movement pattern.

Finally in this chapter, I will tell you about the seven positions down the neck and the spine which are worth knowing about, so that anyone might be able to influence these in a home remedy designed by my great teacher Dr Allan.

Three of these points are found in the neck; the next three are positioned just under the neck, between the shoulder blades and down the spine, while the last one is situated far down the spine in the region of the hip.

This treatment involves a positive and a negative aspect. The positive half of the treatment is done with the right thumb, applied to the left side of the afflicted person. The negative half is done by using the left thumb on the right side of the neck. Only the thumbs should be used — either the right thumb on the left side or the left thumb on the right side.

By doing this we get an energy flow in the spine which brings about a healing force that corrects spinal imbalances. The position of the points are as follows:

—The first place to balance the energy is located down the neck, just a little below the skull axis.

—The second place is halfway down the neck, at the third and fourth cervical vertebra.

—The third place is at the base of the neck, at the seventh cervical vertebra.

—The fourth is situated at just about one inch below the third place, in the region of the first dorsal vertebra.

—The fifth place is in the area of the third dorsal vertebra.

—The sixth place is the fifth dorsal vertebra.

—The seventh and last place is in the region of the lumbar spine.

The correct application of this method only needs two minutes. Take a deep breath before the treatment starts and continue to breathe normally. Do not apply any pressure as only slight contact with the ball of the thumb is needed. In all spinal conditions one will get relief from these palpations and they may prove very useful if no immediate help from a practitioner is available. It may also be done at home in between professional treatments, in accordance with the practitioner's instructions.

I will now move on to the lumbar spine area, which is dealt with in the next chapter.

7

The Lumbar Spine

I SUPPOSE THAT the greatest percentage of spinal problems
we come across in our practice are related to the lumbar spine.
From the diagram in this book we see that the lumbar spine
section contains five vertebrae. Often patients come to see me
with what they suspect is a 'slipped disc'. However, with a
lower-back pain, patients might think that a disc has slipped,
but fortunately this is not always the case. Once we look at it
we frequently find that it concerns a less serious problem,
which nevertheless may need attention. Even so, I am often
asked to explain what a slipped disc exactly is.

The symptoms of these lower-back pains vary and are often
due to a general lack of exercise. A sedentary life puts strain on
the lumbar spine if and when exercise is taken. Weakness of
the lumbar spine may also be due to dietary mismanagement.
Incorrect use of the spine may then be the cause of difficulties,
when the patient is sometimes subjected to severe pain and
distress. This pain can involve spasms, stabbing pains, pains
down one or both legs and this altogether can result in a
severely debilitating discomfort; even to the extent that I

have seen patients enter the clinic bent double to an unbelievable degree.

Many of these lower-back pains or, if worse, sciatica, relate
to degenerative joints disease. In bad cases, it is usually due to
a fracture or an infection. It is worse, however, if it is caused by
a tumour or spina bifida. Back pains may also occur because of
obesity or during pregnancy, when the weight distribution
temporarily alters and therefore the back is put under stress.

Any back complaint deserves a thorough examination
before the practitioner can make up his mind as to what is
wrong, and to this purpose X-rays should be taken. However,
when one has been in practice for many years, by checking the
loss of reflexes or sensory changes, one can quite often find
out quickly where the problem stems from.

Lumbar spinal complaints are sometimes confused with
sciatica pains, but in practice I have found that, fortunately,
there are relatively few cases of sciatica. I will discuss this
condition in more detail in the next chapter.

Rather than sciatica, the complaints are more often cases of
compression or contraction of the spine. Whenever the nerves
are compressed outside the spinal cord an acute pain can
occur.

Afflictions such as lumbago and spinal stenosis can cause
severe problems in the lumbar spine, as can, of course,
arthritic conditions, which I have discussed at length in my
book on rheumatism and arthritis.

These conditions can be eased considerably by an
osteopathic practitioner, even though for acute lower-back
pains bed rest is frequently prescribed by the general
practitioner, with heat applications and/or oral analgesics.
Occasionally traction is prescribed, but it is a grim case when
bed rest for six or eight weeks is prescribed and, unfortunately, the patient often experiences a deterioration of the
condition afterwards. Sometimes the patient is advised to
spend some time in a plaster cast, or in the worst of cases an
operation is recommended as the only way to solve their
problems.

With a sensible approach to these conditions, many of which are often referred to as a 'slipped disc', an operation can often be avoided — and of course any option is preferable to surgery.

What is a slipped disc really? When I am asked this question I usually point out first of all that this name is misleading. I will try to explain in simple terms what this condition is about.

The disc is a strong cartilaginous ring which is firmly attached to the vertebrae on both sides. The inner mass is called the nucleus pulposus. When, possibly due to a traumatic experience, a tear appears in this cartilage, the inner substance can flow out. A comparison I sometimes use in my explanation is that it is like a cream chocolate. When the chocolate covering breaks, the cream oozes out.

If the cartilage is damaged and the fluid of the nucleus pulposus escapes, this results in spasms in the surrounding area. Even worse is when this puts pressure on the nerves, especially when the sciatic nerve is involved. In that case we are dealing with a prolapse of the intervertebral disc. The ability of the disc to act as a shock absorber is then greatly impaired and stiffness, a degree of immobility and severe pain is the result.

Many patients arrive at the clinic with the request for treatment so that the disc will 'click' back into place, as they sincerely believe that it is just a simple matter of manipulating it back into its proper position. If no herniation has occurred this is indeed often possible, but when there is a prolapse of the intervertebral disc, the matter has become much more complicated. Then correction of the spine becomes essential and I intend dealing with the methods available to us for this purpose in the next chapter.

Forceful manipulation must be avoided at any time in such cases and we should never allow ourselves to forget that we are dealing here with some of the finest material of Nature's most intricate design.

Sometimes during manipulative treatment a patient will cry out triumphantly that 'it clicked'. The click which is assumed to have righted the complaint is rarely the answer. This generally is only an innocent crack somewhere in the body and the 'click' is more often a case of wishful thinking, as the disc is more like a gelatinous mass which does not really click. The cartilage acts more or less like a shock absorber or a cushion between the vertebral bodies, so as to help the spinal column to sustain the pressures it is under.

The cartilaginous shapes are protecting the vertebral bodies and provide nourishment for the discs. Therefore it pays to look after them and, although people look at me askance when I point out the importance of a balanced diet to prevent problems, if there is a vulnerability in this particular area, I maintain that diet may be a contributory factor.

Sometimes patients tell me that it was just due to a cough, or that they only stepped off or onto the pavement, when the disc slipped. And indeed sometimes a simple jerk can cause the ligaments of the cartilage to tear, but quite often stress, over-use or degeneration are the factors underlying this problem.

The area in which this condition mostly occurs is, in my experience, the lumbar spine: lumbar vertebrae four and five to sacrum one. Although it is not always quite as drastic, if there is a prolapse of the intervertebral disc, it will strike the nerve roots and the whole area will be plagued by severe pains. If indeed the nerve roots are stricken, then let us be grateful for the science of acupuncture, because with this therapy the painful situation can be eased considerably and almost immediately.

It is, therefore, so unfortunate when patients who have reached their wits' end under these conditions, when they are in constant pain, will agree to surgery. A laminectomy will then be performed, in which it is deemed necessary to either cut or remove the vertebra. However, if the patient can muster up the courage and the patience to undergo some of the treatments which I have previously described, surgery is rarely necessary. I have given these forms of treatment for many years and by doing so it has often been possible to avoid surgery.

An eminent surgeon has been a good friend of mine for many years, but we rarely used to talk shop. Once, however, on returning from one of my trips to China, we had quite an exchange of views and he asked permission to spend some time with me in my clinic, so that he could study first-hand some of the methods we use. His inquisitive attitude rather pleased me and after our stint together he stated that it was about time that surgeons reviewed their thoughts on anatomy.

For a while we did not see each other and then out of the blue, he contacted me. He had a patient whom he would have referred for a laminectomy under normal circumstances. However, after his experiences in our clinic he had given it second thoughts. Between us we decided to give her acupuncture treatment, as he had seen the benefits of this therapy during his visit to the clinic. His consequent reaction was one of gratitude as this young woman finally did not need a laminectomy, because her condition was rectified after several acupuncture treatments.

Let me state again, however, that I do not rule out surgery in every circumstance. In some cases it is indeed the only solution, but it would be wise to first try some of the more gentle alternative methods, and therefore it is sensible to look for help as soon as a problem becomes apparent. Whether the patient is diagnosed as having acute lumbago, muscle spasms, or whichever back complaint, always have it seen to immediately, before the situation deteriorates too far!

If a condition is allowed to linger on, it might create more or less permanent problems. The source of the symptoms might deteriorate further if the condition is not looked at in time, as is often the case with sciatica.

Sciatica might be symptomatic in that it produces pins and needles, but a real sciatica will cause severe pain for the patient. When the pressure on the hypersensitive nerve root becomes worse, treatment is urgently needed. Generally, the patient will be all right again after three to five treatment sessions, while with some exercising, the muscles will get stronger and become capable once more of performing the normal required movements.

Lesions of the lower thoracic and lumbar segments of the spinal column may interfere with the sacro-iliac joint, which restricts the functioning of the nerve and blood supply. subsequently other problems may arise, which especially in females may reveal themselves in circulation problems, or those pertaining to the ovaries and uterus. Very often there will be a disturbance in the regularity of the monthly cycle and unless the source of these problems is found and rectified, the patient will sometimes be made to undergo surgery in this field, where it might not have been necessary.

Poor posture does affect the structural integrity of the spine and therefore it also affects other important organs. The sacro-iliac joint, a lumbo-sacral torsion, will influence the pelvic structure via the nerve supply. Then contraction or compression will often be the case and when such conditions occur, the patient will sometimes complain about having to urinate more frequently than would normally be the case.

A sciatica patient with lower-back problems should take great care to avoid constipation. I remember a public lecture I gave one evening which I largely devoted to back and neck complaints. At the end of my talk an elderly lady, who was in her nineties and sitting in the front row, asked if she was allowed to make a remark. She told us that she was a retired nurse and had worked for an orthopaedic surgeon for a long period of time. He had always made a point of reminding his staff to impress on patients that they should steer clear of constipation. In the olden days castor oil was used for this purpose. Nowadays there are fortunately other means available, equally effective, but rather more palatable than castor oil.

I was quite happy with her interruption, because it confirmed that any contributory factors should be eliminated.

I once read an interesting report by a group of surgeons about the possibilities for eliminating pains which stemmed from the discs. Some surgeons favoured local anaesthetics to extinguish the pain, while others preferred injections of saline into the disc, thereby raising the pressure in the area. I have said it before and will say it again . . . Compare it to throwing a pebble into the water. The pebble affects one small area briefly, but the consequent ripples on the water will affect a much larger area for a very much longer period of time!

In my opinion magnetic therapy is one of the finest ways of restoring the balance in the lumbar region. It often pays to measure the patient's legs and by doing so an imbalance may be found when attempting to square the heels with the patient in a supine position. We will generally find that whenever the legs have been balanced with the help of magnetic therapy, the problems will have been solved, thus proving that stabilisation of the disc may be the solution.

My friend, Dr Bodgener, once told me that with every case of sciatica he had treated, he had noticed that the fifth dorsal vertebra would be particularly sensitive. Before doing anything else, he would always treat the fifth dorsal area first, which would immediately relieve the pressure on the lumbar vertebrae. With the integration of the magnetic field he often succeeded in solving the patient's problems.

The numerous patients with lumbar spinal conditions I have treated have responded favourably to magnetic therapy treatment, which can be adapted to individual requirements. I aim at relieving the pain at the first possible opportunity which, though not always easy, is, thanks to these particular methods, most successful.

In front of me I have a letter written by a clergyman. Due to a sudden movement while delivering an impassioned sermon, he suffered a slipped disc. He underwent numerous treatments at many different places and he eventually arrived at my clinic. From his letter I quote:

> I am simply writing to express my gratitude for the effective treatment I received at your clinic. I very much regret that alternative medicine is not more highly regarded by the medical authorities, and for that matter by the general public. It definitely offers many positive facts and options. It was my

pleasure to have met you and to have been treated with such courtesy and patient concern.

On the other hand I am equally pleased with the letter from a well-known surgeon written to his patient, who also happened to be a patient at our clinic. From this letter I quote:

It has come to my attention that you are receiving alternative treatment from Dr de Vries and this seems to me the best management at present. Although my understanding of your problem is sympathetic, I nonetheless feel that your back problem as such is virtually impossible to approach from a surgical standpoint. I also feel that the benefits obtained under the care of Dr de Vries at the moment, could not be enhanced by any treatment of mine.

Such letters are heartwarming and encourage the realisation that the value of complementary medicine is not always misunderstood.

One of the most difficult situations to treat are sacro-iliac lesions and I fully agree with the surgeon who wrote to me: 'The sacro-iliac joint still mystifies me and I am not alone in that in my profession. I would like the opportunity to work with you for a while and study your approach to problems relating to this joint.'

In a book published in 1915 I read that one of the earliest discoveries by the founder of osteopathy was that the sacro-iliac joint is a freely movable articulation and therefore subject to subluxation, which means sprain or partial dislocation. This joint had been regarded as immovable by anatomists, but later, Sir Richard Quain, a well-known British surgeon, called attention to the manner in which the sacrum was suspended between the iliums. The sacro-iliac articulation was decided to be slightly movable and was classified among these joints.

The founder of osteopathy, Dr A. T. Still, had been adjusting subluxations of the innominates or hip bones and, fully ten years after he taught the osteopathic methods of correcting subluxations, followers of the regular school of medicine began research into the action of this joint.

Yet, even today, the sacro-iliac joint or sacro-iliac lesions still give us some mystifying problems. I have found, however, that these particular complaints do react very well to acupuncture and laser treatment.

If help is not immediately available when lower-back pain occurs, some simple hints, which can be adopted at home, may come in useful. These are as follows:

—If the pain is very acute and frequent, short periods of bed rest are suggested. It is best to lie on the abdomen with two pillows placed under the stomach. Breathe in slowly through the nose, into the stomach and breathe out through the mouth.

—Do not sleep on a soft bed or on any soft surface. Either sleep on the floor or place a board under the mattress.

—Try not to bend forward.

—With acute pains, apply an ice pack or an ice-cold cloth to the area.

—Stand as erect and balanced as possible.

—Take short walks if possible, but keep as erect a posture as you can.

—Always sit on a straight-backed hard chair.

—When rising in the morning first crawl on hands and knees, with both arms fully extended. Rock body forwards and backwards, trying to loosen up.

—Avoid undue lifting or bending.

—Try walking short distances, gentle swimming or cycling, if at all possible.

—Do some of the exercises as outlined in the Appendix.

8

Lumbar Spine Complaints

Neuritis

NEURITIS is an inflamed irritation of the nerves, which can cause severe pains, causing the majority of victims to turn to a painkiller. They will find, however, that this brings only temporary relief, as the inflammation will continue, resulting in yet more tissue pain.

The danger exists that if neuritis is allowed to continue unchecked, more serious problems can develop. If proper treatment is given in adjusting the spine and the adjacent tissue, resulting in improved nerve transmission and tissue balance, healing of the inflamed areas will be spontaneous.

In order to affect a cure, the cause of the inflammation must be located and treated. It is quite a normal reaction to any disorder, such as an infection or a swelling, for an inflammation to rear its head. I have found one of the finest remedies for such conditions to be Arnica, and that indeed is the flower which is featured on the cover of this book.

Very often the muscle tissue which is controlled by the nerve is under so much pressure that the area of pain may be

72

atrophied or wasted from lack of nutrition or lack of use. Again, this condition should be treated without delay.

The pains due to neuritis may attack not only the legs, or the lumbar spine, but can and do also attack arms, wrists, shoulders, fingers, etc. To be free of this nerve pain is a considerable relief for the patient, because when inflammation diminishes, the healing can begin. In such cases we have achieved good results by neural therapy injections into specific trigger points.

Whenever the cause of neuritis or an inflammation is treated, the condition will improve. Sometimes this can be done by corrective manipulation, shortwave Diapulse treatment, acupuncture or laser treatment. We have quite a choice of therapies available to us these days, which are all equally effective in their own fields.

Neuritis or neuralgia, which can also be related to spinal problems, should be treated, as the nerves are stricken almost immediately and the pain can be very intense and deep-seated. These pains should not go unchecked or untreated, as in today's society we are all subjected to much stress. Lower-back pains are especially incapacitating while driving. As we all tend to overload our muscular system it is always advisable to seek help. After careful examination, electro-acupuncture treatment to the tender points may be given, which usually brings a measure of relief.

While preparing this chapter I was consulted by an elderly patient who was experiencing some rather drastic osteophytic changes in the lower lumbar spine. He had been prescribed a wide variety of medicine by the various practitioners he had decided to consult. This had rather disturbed him, however, and I therefore decided to avoid any oral medication for the time being and opted instead for acupuncture treatment. This I followed with laser treatment and some time later, after a discussion, I decided to prescribe Symphosan as a back-up oral medication. The lower-back pain was very much reduced after the first treatment and it was heartening to see the progress in the patient's walking. We managed to get his neuritis pains under control and he was thrilled that despite his age he regained his mobility.

Sciatica
As mentioned in the previous chapter, this is a particularly nasty condition. Sciatica is mostly treated in our clinic with acupuncture and/or laser treatment, topped up occasionally by interferential treatment. Sometimes sciatica patients find benefit from the homoeopathic remedy Imperarthritica, which is conducive to gaining control over inflammation. Some patients also react well to a substantial dose of Arnica.

I quote from a letter which I received from the husband of a lady who consulted me in connection with sciatica:

> Following my wife's visit to your clinic last Thursday, I am delighted to be able to report that she thoroughly enjoyed our daughter's twenty-first birthday celebrations at the weekend. She was able to join in to a much greater extent than would have been possible had she not attended your clinic. Your prompt treatment turned what could have been a disaster for us into a most pleasurable occasion for everyone.

This lady's sciatica pains were caused by intervertebral protrusion on the nerve root. She was very nervous and uptight initially and, after having put her at ease, I managed to alleviate the pressure on the nerve which caused a tremendous change for the better.

Spinal Stenosis
Another condition which I would like to discuss is spinal stenosis, which is a less common form of sciatica. This condition occurs where there is a contracture of the spine and this creates pressure on the surrounding structures. It resembles a vascular disease in that it stimulates intermittent claudication.

Spinal stenosis is a complicated condition to treat because it involves the sciatic nerve roots. It causes considerable pain in the buttocks, thighs and calves, which creates particular problems when climbing stairs, Claudication, which is the impairment of the circulation, causes the patient to tire quickly because of the prolonged and persistent pains. These patients usually react well to enzyme therapy, which is recommended to be followed in combination with a good, balanced diet.

The enzyme therapy Rheumajecta aims to lend elastic support to blood vessels and nerves and to detoxicate serum permeating through the connective tissue into the parenchyma. Connective tissue accompanies blood vessels and nerves right down to the · smallest branches in the muscles and other organs.

Lumbago

Another condition which is very often misunderstood is lumbago. Often, back problems are erroneously referred to by this name. Lumbago is a painful condition of the lumbar muscles caused by inflammation of the fibrous sheaths. Not infrequently, lumbago will also affect the urinary tracts and although this disorder mostly reacts rather well to osteopathic treatment, I personally prefer to prescribe a good kidney remedy in acute and painful cases. Acupuncture also, by concentrating on the specific kidney points, will often ease lumbago pains quickly.

The remedy I most often prescribe under these conditions is kidney drops, called Nephrosolid, from the Dr Vogel Bioforce range. This is a fresh herb preparation which helps to stimulate kidney function, relieve kidney and bladder problems, and increase urinary discharge. It contains the following ingredients:

Solidago virgaurea	E. Golden Rod
Potentilla anserina	Silverweed
Betula alba	Birch
Ononis spinosa	Restharrow
Viola tricolor	Wild pansy
Polygonum aviculare	Knotweed
Equisetum arvense	Horsetail
Juniperus communis	Juniper

The patient will usually be able to notice the first signs of relief within a couple of days.

Sacro-iliac Slip

Among the many types of lower-back disorders, there is the condition of spasms and pulling of the muscle tendons, resulting in misalignment of the pelvic parts because of a sacro-iliac condition.

With a sacro-iliac complaint or imbalance the best results I have had were obtained with acupuncture and laser treatment, followed up by Symphosan and/or Urticalcin.

A regular quantity of Silicea is also advantageous and gentle manipulation — unless there is an arthritic condition present in the sacro-iliac joint. More often than not the balance will be restored, to the patient's delight.

Spina Bifida

Spina bifida patients should be treated with great caution and, personally, I rule out manipulation because of their generally precarious condition. This affliction concerns a congenital malformation of the spine, due to the neural arch of one or more vertebrae failing to fuse. This defect, when present, occurs most frequently in the lumbar sacral region. Although some mild spina bifida cases react reasonably well to palpation, I prefer to use magnetic treatment, acupuncture and/or laser therapy.

In cases where spina bifida is present to a lesser degree I have also found that it has paid to use the German remedy Araniforce. This works marvellously well to combat the pains and is a mixture of several homoeopathic extracts. Also recommended is the Dr Vogel remedy Galeopsis, an extract of *Galeopsis segetum* or the hemp nettle. Finally I would prescribe a Silicea compound for these conditions.

A young girl who suffers from spina bifida recently returned to the clinic and with tears in her eyes she thanked me over and over again for the relief she had experienced after following this advised course of treatment.

Spina bifida patients would be wise to carefully consider the suitability of any exercises, as their movement ability is restricted and over-strenuous or wrong exercising could result in a deterioration of their general health.

Arthritic Lumbar Spine

Those people who regularly suffer from arthritic pains in the lumbar area would do well to check if their diet supplies them with the required ingredients. Acupuncture treatment is often suitable for them, as well as certain homoeopathic remedies which I have described in detail in my book on rheumatism and arthritis.

One of my patients, who is a distinguished member of the High Court, underwent treatment along these lines at our clinic and reacted very favourably to it. From a letter he wrote me, I read: 'I have not felt so well for quite some time. Once again I feel like a complete human being.'

With any lumbar spine condition, I advise caution with lifting, bending or any sudden movements. Physical fitness is important as long as one is sensible about it and gentle exercise is taken. This will enable the person concerned to build up and increase the healing power.

Coccyx

The other subject I intend to discuss here is the coccyx — made up of four little crystal forms, located at the bottom of the lumbar spine. Despite their limited size, they are of great importance. Like the atlas they will affect the whole of the spine and I have found that when I treat the atlas with the laser, the coccyx, as well as the whole of the spine, will relax.

The coccyx is rather tender and vulnerable and is therefore easily bruised, when it can become the cause of considerable discomfort. A fall in slippery conditions, or an accidental stumble down the stairs, can easily damage the coccyx and then the pains may affect the whole of the spine.

In the treatment of sciatica I have been able to relieve the pain by very gentle manipulation of the coccyx and the area underneath. By gentle adjustment palpation the tailbone will relax, encouraging the reflexes in the whole of the body to slacken.

Those people who have suffered from coccydynia, which is a medical term for persistent pain in the coccyx, will know only too well what I am talking about when I say that any damage to these small crystals is far-reaching in its effects on one's mobility. The only way to relieve pain in that area is to try and bring about relaxation from the atlas at the top of the spine, down to the lowest part of the coccyx. In cases of coccydynia stress can be eased by Symphosan. Gentle manipulation can then be given which will bring welcome relief.

I remember that years ago Dr Leonard Allan, the writer of the foreword to this book, taught his students that:

—pain on motion is a sensory pain and the anterior body zones are all involved;

—pain on pressure is a motor pain and is of sympathetic origin;

—motor pain is of a sympathetic origin;

—sensory pain is of a para-sympathetic nature.

We also know that the hypothalamus, a gland lying on the third ventricle of the brain and linked with the pituitary gland, is an active factor where pain is involved. Therefore it is logical to consider this gland and endeavour to relax this area in painful conditions.

Fortunately, man possesses an innate force which directs and controls the entire course of life, and which will heal afflictions and ailments if it is transported and directed in a correct balance.

No healing can take place unless relaxation has been inspired, so it is important under these conditions that, wherever possible, tension should be avoided or minimised in order to speed up the process of improvement. The muscles in particular will react immediately to strain and tension and this should therefore be prevented.

I will recap briefly on important points to remember. It is the muscles which move the bones; bones do not move without muscles and the more relaxed the muscles are, so much the better. Then contraction of the muscles which trigger nerve impulses will be reduced and the neck and back conditions are alleviated.

9

Osteoporosis

OSTEOPOROSIS is a condition of bone fragility, due either to reabsorption of calcium or a decrease in bone-tissue mass where the remaining bone is still quite normal. This condition may be caused by dietary deficiencies, fractures or possibly as a result of long-term use of cortisone. If, as is often the case with a primary osteoporosis, there is increased bone absorption, although the bone formation may appear quite normal, some defective bone formation may exist.

This condition is more prevalent in women than in men and usually occurs during middle age or affects the older generation.

Secondary osteoporosis can be induced by several medical conditions, such as a multiple myeloma, a partial gastorectomy or by too much hydrocortisone in the body.

While some patients with osteoporosis will experience inconvenience or pain, others may be free of such symptoms. If, however, any pain is present, it might be acute, especially on the weight-bearing part of the spine — the dorsals 8 and 9.

Compression or contraction of the spine may often be

experienced or a dorsal kyphosis may develop, which could result in a cervical lordosis causing considerable pain in the dorsal or lumbar area. Especially in the older generation, osteoporosis can prove to be a considerable handicap, one which needs to be treated with great care.

A deformity of the spine can generally be recognised fairly easily by a slight wedging or an apparently gentle bend. The bones may have worn rather thin and fragile and therefore expert care is recommended and indeed necessary.

Quite frequently during an acute backache, especially if a fracture exists, abnormal stress and compression in the spine is experienced. Generally, drugs, the drinking of lots of milk, increased quantities of vitamin D, oral calcium, oestrogen and a well-balanced dietary composition are considered the best treatment for this affliction. In severe cases other hormonal preparations may be introduced together with sodium fluoride, but sometimes this may result in more serious side-effects than the initial complaints for which the treatment was designed.

It may, therefore, be advisable, especially when the bones have become increasingly brittle, that a more gentle approach be taken in cases of severe osteoporosis.

Firstly, a sensible diet is necessary. The consumption of food with a high calcium content is advantageous and the use of Dr Vogel's Urticalcin, a homoeopathic combination of calcium and silicic acid, has often paid off handsomely in such cases.

I always find that the use of compound vitamins, minerals and trace elements is desirable. In homoeopathy we are fortunate in that we have the very worthwhile remedy Araniforce at our disposal, which is invaluable in the treatment of any degenerative process of the bone structure. Araniforce has proven to be of particular help in the rebuilding of tissue with many of my patients. This German remedy, made by Messrs Vogel & Weber, has been considered a real blessing by many of its users and I never fail to notice the encouraging results when I prescribe it.

I cannot stress sufficiently how wonderful a friend Nature is. Let us consider the composition of Araniforce for instance, which contains:

alchemilla	*equisetum*
calamus arom.	*ilex*
calcium carbonicum	*silicea*
calcium phosphoricum	*symphytum*

as well as some vitamin B preparations. The end result is a remedy which gives us a safe and efficient form of treatment without fear of side-effects.

Neural therapy has also served many patients well, especially when they were suffering from acute pains.

A general misunderstanding exists that patients with osteoporosis should take large quantities of calcium. This, however, is only absorbed in the blood in minute proportions if taken as a single preparation. In many cases, vitamin D is introduced to assist calcium absorption and over the years it has been found that Urticalcin in combination with a fresh nettle extract will greatly assist the calcium absorption in the bloodstream, from which patients will obtain more benefit.

We should not underestimate silicium preparations. Silicea, depending which form is prescribed and used, can be of the greatest help to an osteoporosis patient. This silicic acid preparation performs a very important function for the organs involved. The metabolic system, in its function to the tissue, supplies a water combination with protein content which facilitates the action of silicium.

My recommendation, therefore, for the treatment of this difficult condition is that some good remedies be used in combination with a sensible diet. It is important that the patient realises that every part of the bone structure, from the skull to the ribs and the spine, has its own function to perform when the body has been hit by osteoporosis.

I clearly remember an elderly gentleman who was shown

into my consulting-room one afternoon. He really looked poorly and was visibly suffering from severe pains. I examined his spine, which proved to be in poor condition and, although I had not seen any X-rays, I realised that his condition was quite serious. He told me that he had been receiving cortisone treatment for a long spell and although he was not aware of any benefits gained from this, he had been informed that there was no other option.

As I could clearly see how much pain his condition was causing him, I was hesitant to treat him and decided instead to prescribe something to ease the pain. I strongly advised him to see his own doctor, however, as I felt that further treatment was called for. When consulted, his own doctor also recognised the need for specialised treatment and arranged to have him admitted to hospital the very next day.

Unfortunately, during his second day at the hospital he fell. This, as well as a fall which had taken place a few weeks previously in which he had quite seriously damaged his spine in two places, resulted in X-rays showing fractured discs of dorsals 8 and 9. The severe discomfort he had been suffering previously, in addition to the newly sustained fractures, led to his death shortly afterwards.

I do feel, however, that if this particular person, who was on long-term cortisone treatment, had been given correct counselling and had then taken precautions in his dietary management and used some of the above-mentioned remedies, the outcome may have been different. At any time we must remember that prevention is always better than a cure!

On the other hand, I remember a middle-aged lady, who was lucky enough to be able to stop the cortisone treatment after sensible counselling. She was suffering severe pains and found great relief in homoeopuncture. Not only was she able to discontinue the cortisone treatment, but her osteoporosis condition also showed a marked improvement. In a letter she wrote me she stated:

I am so happy to tell you that for the past few weeks I have not had any pain worth mentioning. In fact, I feel better than I have done for the last four years and want to thank you from the bottom of my heart for all your help during the past year. I shall not hesitate to get in touch if any symptoms were to reappear.

Close co-operation and a relationship of trust between patient and practitioner usually pays good dividends. With correct treatment and wholehearted commitment on the patient's behalf, much can be achieved. Let us, however, always keep in mind that Nature is the ultimate healer.

10

Osteomyelitis

DURING A PARTICULARLY busy surgery one morning, a lady who had flown over from Ireland was shown into my room. She wished to see me to find out if anything could be done about the pains which plagued her constantly and about her restricted movement, which was becoming increasingly bothersome.

It did not take me long to diagnose that this lady was suffering from osteomyelitis, which is an inflammation of the bone marrow.

While I listened to her story about how her hopes had been raised and dashed several times over when a new therapy or approach had been recommended, I kept an open mind on which treatment would be most suitable. I carefully considered her condition, but felt that we might have problems establishing a trusting relationship as she had been disappointed several times previously. Nevertheless, I needed her trust and confidence to be able to work with her, and a half-hearted approach could be considered a waste of time.

However, as we talked I realised that her hopes had not been totally squashed and I recognised a willingness to follow my advisory guidelines.

Osteomyelitis is mostly due to an infection of the bone and/or marrow. This can be caused by either a positive or negative bacteria, a fungus or other infection. Whatever the reason, it can result in a very unpleasant condition for the patient who is attacked by it.

When the infection reaches the bone, multiple abscesses throughout the whole body may appear, which can be seen as part of a general infection. Sometimes a fall or a minor injury may subsequently result in open wounds.

Mostly, this condition first attacks the bone marrow, causing damage to the marrow cavity. Then a mixed infection situation will be the result.

In the case of my Irish patient the infections were present near some of the joints and the knee joints in particular were very inflamed, with the spin-off effect of swellings on the synovial membrane. An increase in the joint's fluid had enlarged her knees incredibly. Because of the time which had passed, the chronic, deep-seated infection had done unbelievable damage to the whole area. In one way, however, she had been fortunate, because when the early orthodox treatment had not done much to improve her condition, she had adopted a new approach to the affliction and changed her dietary management. Some friends had passed on some useful information and this had enabled her to cope reasonably, despite the tenderness, pains and limitations.

Not only was the condition of osteomyelitis diagnosed in this patient, but she was also rather rheumatic. She had lost a good deal of weight and also suffered other spinal complaints. She told me that she had been given very little hope. As the orthodox treatment had shown few benefits, if any, she was prepared to do anything which was deemed necessary in the hope of even the slightest sign of improvement.

The greatest problem I could foresee and which I had to tackle first of all was to try and deal with the abscesses which had formed beneath the cortex of the bone. I decided to use some strong enzyme injections to help ease this situation. Once again I fell back on Rheumajecta and Vasolastine. Both enzyme injections are produced in the Netherlands, and they have always stood me in good stead in difficult cases when treating infections or abscesses.

I doubt if a straightforward antibiotic would have been any help, but was certainly grateful for the availability of Echinaforce, which is a natural antibiotic from Dr Vogel's range of Bioforce products.

As this patient had already adopted certain dietary restrictions herself, I now had to adapt these guidelines to her specific complaints, which slightly confused her initially.

My advice to her was to eat plenty of fresh vegetables and fruit and to remove pork, spices, refined sugar and flour etc. from her diet, as well as any foods in which these ingredients are used.

Fortunately the patient was not a smoker and this was to her credit. Smoking is always detrimental to one's health, but specifically so in the case of an osteomyelitis patient.

I started the treatment with large doses of Echinaforce, Urticalcin and Galeopsis — a silicic acid preparation. Afterwards I prescribed increased doses of Echtrosept, which is a remedy made by the German company Vogel & Weber, containing the following:

Apis mell.
Bryonia
Echinacea
Eupatorium
Lachesis (snake's poison)
Thuja

in addition to some homoeopathic substances.

She was extremely excited when, after only a brief period, she started to notice the first signs of improvement. The progress persisted and she regained most of her movement ability and was eventually able to travel by herself from Ireland to our clinic, where she received a course of acupuncture treatment for her arthritic condition.

Although she had been told that she could not expect to ever get better, she had refused to give up hope and she finally benefited from her stubbornness. Her problems these days are minimal and nothing compared to what it was like during the previous years. She asked me in a letter: 'I just cannot believe this. How is this at all possible? Will this last?'

Well, it has now lasted for quite a few years already and the lady in question is still doing very well. Due to her overwhelming gratitude she has referred quite a few people from Ireland to me, who have become patients and who often talk of her as a living example of what can be achieved with alternative medicine.

Basically, conditions relating to infections, viruses, abscesses, etc. give us the clearest signals that Nature is our best healer.

I remember a young patient with a similar problem. Unfortunately, with the younger generation it is often much more difficult to get the message of the dietary approach across. Very often we know beforehand that they were not taking it seriously enough and will break the regime whenever it suits them. It is, however, very important, as with any form of treatment, that dietary instructions are strictly adhered to, as these are designed to ward off and avoid the risks of these conditions taking hold in the first place or check the progress of existing conditions.

It is interesting to witness the value of such programmes, especially in the younger generation, if they *are* prepared to follow the guidelines without deviation. In severe cases it is advisable to adopt organically grown foods in the dietary regime, along with some of the previously mentioned remedies, in order to effect an improvement in the condition. Although it is not always easy to obtain organically grown foods, if at all possible it will pay to do so, as the enhanced power of Nature will be especially worthwhile.

In my efforts to convince this particular young patient I referred to above, I produced a report which I had only recently obtained, which underlined the importance of organically grown food.

After the nuclear disaster at Chernobyl, much attention was paid to the way radioactivity had affected vegetables, fruit and plants. It was discovered by a group of researchers, with the help of a Geiger counter, that organically grown foods were less affected than those foods produced and fertilised with the aid of chemical substances. Vegetables, fruit and plants grown in natural compost were thus eliminated from the list of produce which was radioactively contaminated long before the foods produced with chemical fertilisers were cleared.

Radioactivity from the cosmos is known over the whole earth. Under normal circumstances the borderline of safety on a Geiger counter is 17 pm. If the Geiger counter produces a higher figure, then that produce is not considered safe for consumption. Where a Geiger counter was used on chemically fertilised foods, the readings sometimes went up as high as 200 pm, whilst on organically grown produce this figure only reached 30 pm, where it comes close to toleration. It is therefore of great importance to realise that where the tissue is involved, the syrup-like plant juices can serve as a protective device.

We all know that it is difficult, if not impossible, to protect ourselves from nuclear fall-out, or, even worse, from nuclear explosions. We do, however, have the knowledge that it is possible to adopt certain protective measures in order to minimise some of the effects of radiation.

It is advisable to use kelp, molasses, calcium and vitamin C, as well as a good mineral and vitamin preparation. If osteomyelitis was caused initially by an infection, inflammation or a virus, it is most important that these causes be eliminated, also by these products.

Osteomyelitis can cause quite considerable damage and I remember a case where the patient had open wounds which would not heal. The smell of these wounds was most offensive. Some operative measures had previously been taken for this patient and unfortunately it took a long time before any response was noticeable to the large doses of natural antibiotics and enzyme preparations, which were administered by injection as well as orally. Oil of Evening Primrose capsules were also prescribed, but although the patient progressed, the improvement seemed to be painfully slow.

Patients with osteomyelitis have to adhere very strictly to the prescribed treatment methods, as otherwise it will take a long time before any progress is noticeable. However, once the inflammation of the bone marrow is under control, it can be hoped that this debilitating and difficult condition may be overcome.

11

Sports Injuries

HAVING BEEN APPROACHED, over the years, by many participants of different branches of sport of varying nationalities, among them football players, tennis players, golfers, athletes and jockeys, I have often pondered on the best ways to treat sports injuries. It is a known fact that with a tournament coming up soon, or if an injury occurs during a championship, they need help quickly and effectively.

I have been approached by some famous celebrities, frequently in the latter stages of a championship. This was more often than not by the golfing fraternity, which is not surprising considering that I live in a part of the country which is richly endowed with tournament golf courses. I was then expected to 'fix it by hook or by crook', as I sometimes refer to it, so that he or she was able to continue into the latter stages of the tournament.

There are different ways of dealing with the injuries which affect sports enthusiasts and, to my pleasure, I have received many letters of gratitude and acknowledgement to let me know that they either managed to pull through to the next round, or have even gone on to win the championship.

I am rather proud of the fact that where some sportsmen or women had totally given up, they were enabled to make a comeback, thanks to the many alternative methods available to us. Some of them have even gone on to reach heights in their profession of which they had never considered themselves capable.

When I state that I consider fitness in sport to be of utmost importance, you will immediately say that that is quite logical if the sports player wants to attain the best possible achievement. I, however, approach it from another angle.

If sports players pay proper attention to keeping their bodies in good condition, with the use of a correct training programme and a balanced diet, they will then respond very much more quickly to treatment for whatever traumatic experience they may be involved in.

Those who play sports should be fit and healthy. It should not be the case that this fitness is only applicable to enable them to perform in their specific branch of sport. It is common knowledge that fitness is important for one's general stamina. Therefore it is even more important that people who perform sports pay attention to their dietary necessities, to prepare their bodies as well as possible for the heavy demands to which they are subjected. Fortunately, the awareness of this is growing, as the price for lack of or insufficient training or preparation is high.

The key to this is the knowledge that the spine controls to a very large extent the functions of the body, and therefore it deserves to be treated with great care and respect.

Any abnormality in the spine can have detrimental effects on the nervous system, which is responsible for relaying messages from muscles and other tissue to and from the brain. Thus it is a necessity for anyone taking part in sports that the pelvis is properly aligned and the balancing muscles, anterior and posterior, are of normal length and good strength. The upper part of the spine, as well as the neck and shoulders, should be in the correct position to facilitate correct breathing, thereby promoting a good relationship between the different muscle groups.

It is most disturbing to see certain parts of the human body being neglected or overlooked. This is frequently the case with amateur sports players. Postural training is always important and the neck, shoulders and spine should be as straight as possible. If necessary, advice on corrective exercises should be sought.

Breathing exercises enable the spine to find its natural suspension. A sensible and regular exercise programme will maintain the spine and keep the postural muscles in good order. Every sports player should be, and usually is, aware of the fact that an injury is always a possibility. If they have some knowledge of the body's correct physical functions, protracted traumatic experiences may be avoided or minimised.

There are many ways available to us nowadays to enable us to look after the spine, for example keep-fit classes, weight training sessions, yoga classes or gymnastics. Anybody in the sports and athletic world, however, would be wise to have their spine looked at from time to time.

Specific branches of sport attract more amateurs than others and this seems particularly true of jogging, running or aerobics. Frequently, though, insufficient or inadequate training or coaching is given, which often leads to a full waiting-room for the manipulative therapist. Definitely in the rugby, golf or football world, amateur as well as professional, we come across injuries which could have been avoided if enough training was given.

There is much discussion of injuries in all branches of sport, and I have given many lectures on the subject. It is equally important to players and coaches alike to understand properly the workings of the spine in particular, as well as the whole of the body. There is rarely any need to rest for several weeks after an injury if proper treatment is available and if professional advice is adhered to.

Many traumatic symptoms of sports injuries will react quickly and favourably if Arnica is taken. This is one of the finest remedies for the sports player to always have at hand and it should be taken immediately on an injury taking place. *NB* It is important to note that Arnica should *never* be applied to broken skin.

Also the sports player or athlete should be alert if any suspected damage has occurred to the neck. Spinal damage can lead to severe and lasting problems if it is not properly attended to. Self-treatment can sometimes be necessary, but it is always advisable, if at all possible, to contact a doctor, osteopath, physiotherapist or chiropractor. In my practice I have seen many neglected cases which, if they had been treated properly in the first instance, would never have led to the problems these patients suffered in later life.

It is the player's responsibility if he or she decides to abuse their body and fails to pay attention to seemingly minor injuries. Too often it is decided that an ice-pack, or running some really cold water on the injured part will do the trick. This may be so in some cases, but if there is a real problem, professional attention is needed as soon as possible after the occurrence.

In any game or sport it is deemed necessary to take certain risks — a fact which anyone participating in sports is familiar with. The more relaxed a player is when turning out for an event, or for his or her team, the more able they will be to relax their body when entering a critical moment of play. Needless to say this takes nothing away from the concentration. The knowledge of optimum physical fitness will instil a certain confidence in the player.

I have often admired some of the famous sports personalities I have been asked to treat for their ability to relax themselves. It is always reassuring to hear how they managed to keep their heads and maintain control in moments of crisis.

Before I discuss a few of the more common injuries for which I have treated sports players, I will stress again that prevention is better than cure. Therefore some Arnica should always be at hand in case of an injury, no matter how minor it may seem at the time. Always try to keep as calm as possible, as stress can be the cause of more damage than necessary and can also inflict additional tension on the player.

Several times already I have mentioned that bones do not move of their own volition. It is muscle which moves the bone. While bones are rigid, it is the tissue lining of the bones which meets at different joints. The fibrous tissue and fibrous thickenings, called ligaments, are meant to stabilise muscles and tendons in a harmonious manner. In the case of an injury these functions can and will cause structural damage and although the pain at that particular moment may not seem too drastic, swelling and bruising will immediately influence and restrict the normal functioning.

Immediately after an injury occurs, a disturbance is created in the harmonious play between brain, nerves and spinal cord. Nerve impulses will disturb the co-ordination of the function of the muscles. Reflexes will automatically be disturbed if there is any displacement or injury. No matter where the injury occurs, bleeding often takes place, even if it is not visible. It is necessary, if no immediate help is available, to try and stem the bleeding, either with ice-cold water, by applying pressure or with some harmless but effective homoeopathic remedies.

Of course, whenever there are signs of bleeding during an injury, it is advisable to raise the limb to try and stem the flow. I have dealt with many knee, ankle, wrist and elbow injuries where some form of compression should have been applied immediately on suffering the injury.

From experience, I maintain that with knee and ankle injuries acupuncture is the quickest way to relieve the pain and regain mobility. Mostly I follow up this treatment with a homoeopathic injection and possibly with some external application of Symphosan, which I have mentioned before. Symphytum ointment may also be used successfully to soothe the injured area.

Should a knee or ankle be very swollen, I will not hesitate to recommend the old-fashioned remedy of placing a kaolin poultice or a cabbage leaf on alternate nights on the affected area. One evening a kaolin poultice should be bandaged onto the part and kept on overnight and the next evening a cabbage leaf should be used. After that, again use a kaolin poultice — to be continued until the swelling has subsided. This may be regarded as an old wives' tale, but generally the results are better than would be obtained by some of the more modern methods.

As so many footballers in particular seem to have problems with their Achilles tendon, it is good to know how well this injury reacts to acupuncture. Neural therapy, which has been outlined before, is also very helpful for this condition, and sometimes a supportive strapping is advised. One should, however, be careful if supportive strapping is used for long periods of time and always make sure that the muscle fitness is not interfered with. Needless to say, it is important to keep the muscles fit and in working order. With any muscle weakness a very broad spectrum of vitamin B is generally helpful.

With any abrasions, broken skin, cuts or wounds, a good disinfectant has to be used, together with Symphosan tincture, which always has a marvellous healing effect.

Many of the sports players I encounter experience hamstring problems. These muscles are situated on the back of the thigh. Injury often leads to temporary withdrawal of the player, or even retirement. Over the years I have been experimenting to discover how to induce the speediest of recovery for hamstring injuries. Especially with footballers, I have often been called upon to treat injuries to the hamstring tendons and muscles. I did find that these people are best served by acupuncture and moxabustion. Acupuncture in the first instance is very helpful, but during my studies in China I learned that moxabustion influence on the needles tremendously increased the beneficial effects of acupuncture in these particular injuries.

Moxabustion is a well-known method in China. The herbal

mixture used creates a pleasant penetrating influence on the acupuncture point which greatly relaxes the patient. Prof. C. Tsang, one of my most impressive acupuncture teachers, taught me how to place some of the needles locally on the affected part as soon as possible after injury. On the needle we then use moxabustion — a mixture of herbs — or sometimes we may use the leaves of the mugwort. When placing this herb directly with the needle on the affected part, the effect is immediately noticeable from the facial expression of the patient, which shows instant relief. This procedure, however, should only be practised by an experienced acupuncturist.

It is also advisable to follow such treatment with some ultra-sound treatment. This is an application of beamed vibratory energy to the acupuncture meridian system and has been found safe and effective. The method offers several advantages over needle acupuncture and is easily accepted by the patient. It has especially proven its worth in cases of muscular skeletal conditions.

I frequently use this method in combination with acupuncture and this is especially beneficial in elbows, knees, joints and muscles. Since this field encompasses so many entities, lengthy discussions have taken place as to how this method may be used by, for example, the physiotherapist on duty at football matches.

Muscle injuries, tears, pulls, strains, in fact any traumatic experience of this kind reacts beneficially and almost immediately to laser treatment. I have found with the laser, which I now use increasingly, that results are often instantaneously noticeable from the reaction of the person undergoing treatment. It proves how quickly the fibres in the connective tissue will relax, even if the practitioner is in doubt as to whether there is a tear.

A common problem with sports people is an injury to the groin muscle. Often the tissue of the quadriceps muscles has suffered, due to a bad fall or kick and action should be taken immediately. This uncomfortable condition reacts well to Diapulse treatment, to be followed afterwards by laser treatment. It is important to be able to relax this particular area and this may be achieved by some exercises, specifically breathing exercises.

One often finds that these problems go hand-in-hand with cramp, stiffness and pain, and it is sensible if players use some vitamin E in combination with kelp tablets. This will often ease any cramp satisfactorily and quickly.

Similarly, if the fibula or tibia is strained, quick relief can be found by soaking feet and legs in a hot bath to which a handful of bicarbonate of soda has been added. Also beneficial is the use of Symphosan together with some Silicea tablets from the Bioforce range — and I have not only prescribed this for sports players, but also for animals. Horses or dogs also can be helped by Symphosan and Silicea if they have suffered a muscular sprain.

I would also like to add here that in cases of broken or chipped bones, the remedies Galeopsis, Urticalcin and Silicea will increase the healing progress.

When a knee injury is due to torn cartilage, it reacts very well to Dr Vogel's massage oil, which is specifically designed for sports people. I also use this for shoulder and hand injuries.

With any shoulder problem one has to be careful and, nine times out of ten, specialised help is required. Injuries of this kind may result in further complications if no action is taken. Many shoulder problems are caused by a disc lesion and the pressure of a disc on a hypersensitive nerve can lead to muscle spasms. These can be most uncomfortable, but can be relieved with some manipulative treatment. Exercising, however, is also helpful to ease this condition, which can be the cause of much aggravation. Once the cause of the symptoms has been attended to, it is up to the patient to adhere to the advice given. In many cases some extra help is obtained from the use of some homoeopathic remedies.

Energy-giving foods and vitamin supplements are also helpful to recovery in such complaints. In Chapter 12 I will give some general hints and advice on how to keep a healthy spine and the energy needed if one is involved in whatever sport.

Maybe you have heard it before, but I rather like the phrase: 'Movement is life — all life is movement'. Good exercise is necessary, but good balance of energy is equally important!

On many occasions I have been made to recollect my treatment of some of the traumatic injuries some people from the sports world have suffered. I only have to think back to some of the well-known golfers who turned out to become champions, thanks to some corrective manipulative treatment, where appropriate, at the time. This, combined with some simple and natural remedies, was all that was necessary to enable them to continue the tournament.

I have a number of letters in front of me and I quote from one, written by a famous sports personality:

> Thank you so much for fixing my back. I can still remember what it was like before your treatment. Now, whether I walk, sit or play, I feel so much easier. I have thanked you over and over again in my mind, and now I feel that it is high time to do so on paper.
>
> Once again: Many thanks.

Receiving such testimonials acts as a boost and serves to make me more determined to find effective ways of treatment.

I often think, too, of the footballer who had been told to give up the game for good. He had been advised not to expect to ever play the game again. Yet, now I see his name often in the papers and I wonder what would have become of him mentally if he had not received the right treatment — which enabled him to become the outstanding player he is today.

Sometimes I remind my patients of the saying: 'Where there is a will, there is a way'. This adage I much prefer to the following statement: 'You will just have to learn to live with it!' There are now so many methods available to us which can lighten and overcome physical misalignment, malfunctions, injuries or weaknesses, no matter how hopeless the situation may seem at the time.

I remember a player who was badly troubled with an Achilles tendon contracture. This is a restriction of the dorsiflexion of the ankle, resulting in the development of a weak foot and a shortening of the Achilles tendon. He experienced all the familiar symptoms such as calf pain, pain in the lower back and along the longitudinal arch of the foot. He was in a rather poor condition and had been warned that it was unlikely that this problem would ever improve, let alone disappear.

I advised acupuncture, laser treatment and neural therapy for him, which helped tremendously. I also prescribed some homoeopathic remedies and, much to the amazement of his doctors, he restarted training and eventually was declared fit to play again.

Full co-operation and a trusting relationship between the patient and practitioner is essential in such cases, however.

It is some years ago that I was called upon by a rider who had been thrown off his horse, but had been advised that there was nothing wrong with him. Rest had done nothing to cure him. He was, however, in considerable pain due to severe bruising. Again I was extremely pleased to observe the wonderful healing properties of Arnica, that rather insignificant looking plant, which reduced his suffering overnight. It still surprises me every now and then to realise that if we are in tune with Nature, we are in tune with ourselves.

A popular footballer, whom I admire as a person as much as a sporting figure, has, however, given me some anxious moments. He has certainly had his share of misfortune, but recently I received a letter from him, from which I quote:

> Just a short note to express my thanks for everything you did for me during my latest injury. I must admit that there were times when I thought that your confidence in my recovery was misplaced. Fortunately you were correct and I shall always be indebted to you for enabling me to continue to play football.
>
> Wishing you a successful future with the wonderful work you are doing.

Some of my friends in the sporting world have proudly shown me their cups and medals, won after overcoming the odds of injury. It is this challenge in my work — to provide comfort and happiness — which makes me intent on finding ways of successful treatment for other afflictions as well. Too often people have had their hopes raised, only to have them dashed again and we owe it to them to do our utmost to help them.

12

How to Have a Healthy Spine

MANY OF MY regular patients have asked me what they can do to keep their spine in good order. Well, there are quite a few ways in which this can be encouraged, but firstly we must decide what the spine really needs.

In the present day and age our dietary management is so often starved of the proper nutrition, which the spine needs as well as deserves. Thus for the sake of anyone's general health, which includes the spine, *diet* should top the list of general hints and advice as to obtaining and maintaining a correctly functioning spine.

The fact should be recognised that a biochemical mechanism, which enables the body to effect its own repairs, is in need of all the essential elements for this mechanism to function. Our bone structure, encompassing the spine and the vertebrae, requires nutritional elements in sufficient amounts so that the biochemical influence may function during normal nerve transmission. This mechanical interference is necessary for the transmission of nervous energy. This particular aspect is often neglected, but warrants our full attention.

Today, sufficient knowledge is available for us to realise that certain nutritional deficiencies, including insufficient vitamins, minerals and trace elements, will lead to problems. Disturbances which influence our health can often be traced back to a poor diet, i.e. one which lacks the essential nutritional elements.

Proper nutrition is absolutely necessary for the maintenance of a healthy spine and it will also produce the energy which is so badly needed. Many surveys bear out the fact that nowadays a large percentage of the population does not receive that daily requirement and therefore many self-inflicted problems do occur.

Food containing the basic raw materials is needed for the development and maintenance of the vital forces in the body. Sunshine and water are also considered important essentials. A diet with a correct alkaline-acid balance is quite as important as eating the correct proteins and carbohydrates.

With the many patients I treat for back and neck problems, I often notice that incorrect proportions of carbohydrates and proteins have been introduced to a basically healthy diet. For example, during a prolonged protein deficiency we discover that the bone marrow becomes depleted, while the lymphoid tissues and the antibody mechanism will also give cause for concern.

Man is a biochemical as well as a biophysical being and with this in mind we have to realise that the biochemical part of the body functions is in our structural make-up. The framework of body, spine and nerves is alive and will fail to function properly without the required chemistry. Although we can correct the spine, we can never hope to make a good job of it if the nerves are deprived of normal nutritional elements.

It is often wise, therefore, to use supplementary quantities of vitamins, minerals and trace elements where spinal problems exist. Fundamental knowledge of food and its nutritional value and properties is strongly recommended. This does not require mathematical or medical brilliance, but merely common sense. We all ought to eat more of what nature supplies: plenty of raw vegetables or fruit which has not been tampered with. These will contain sufficient quantities of the important minerals such as calcium, iron, magnesium, phosphorus, potassium, sodium and so many others which are required to maintain good health and a properly functioning spine.

In an earlier book, on *Stress and Nervous Disorders*, I have dealt with this subject in detail.

I am often asked to list, in order of importance, what a natural diet should contain. This depends of course very much on the specific needs of that particular person, as each individual's food requirements will vary accordingly. Instead, therefore, I maintain the general guidelines that food should be kept as natural as possible and certain foods should be avoided altogether.

It is because I have treated so many people from every imaginable branch of sport that I have often been asked for advice on this particular subject. Unfortunately, too often insufficient attention is paid to fitness foods during training. These are a must for bodies on which such heavy demands are made.

Sometimes I advise a sports player who is a little bit under the weather to use some honey — and I am looked at as if I had suggested that some kind of poison should be taken. Natural honey is such a wonderful food, however. Not only is it a source of instant energy, but it is of great medicinal value. The vitamins, minerals and trace elements contained in honey may serve as a rapid energy booster. Honey also aids the digestive system.

The same goes for molasses, which in fact contain a rich supply of potassium, serving the sports player as an energy provider. Grains and wheatgerm, which are extremely rich in vitamin E, are also important in the maintenance of good health and a healthy spine.

I remember one sportsman who, although not a spring chicken anymore, still wanted to continue playing football, so I advised him according to what I have stated above. I also recommended that he take two tablets of Dr Vogel's Kelpasan every morning, as this product is rich in iodine, calcium, chlorine, potassium, magnesium, manganese, phosphorus, sodium and sulphur, all of which combine to give the sports player plenty of energy. He most certainly benefited and claimed that he felt as if he had got his 'second wind', which the dictionary explains as 'recovered capacity for continuing any effort'!

'You are what you eat!' We have all heard it said before and this can be seen especially in people who require a lot of physical energy.

This leads us to the next problem — our spine hates obesity. We all know that at a certain weight we feel and perform at our best, i.e. our 'fighting weight'. It is also referred to as our 'efficiency weight' and whatever this weight should be will vary from one person to the other. Even so, we have all had a time in our lives when we knew that we felt comfortable with the weight we carried.

I rather like the expression: 'one ounce of prevention may save a pound of cure' or equally: 'a man should eat to live, not live to eat'. Over-indulgence in food will do nothing whatsoever to aid our efforts to keep a healthy spine. That is certainly borne out by life insurers' records, which show conclusively that obesity is one of the greatest health enemies. Many premature deaths are caused due to excess fat interfering with the metabolism. Weight should be kept under control. Being overweight causes excessive gas in the bowels and we often see patients with back or neck problems where the irritation originates from the spinal nerves as they pass through the intervertebral foramina. With some self-discipline this can be avoided.

This leads to the next question: 'In order to keep obesity under control is it wise to exercise?' My immediate response is affirmative, providing that a sensible exercise programme is followed, as this will also pay dividends in our efforts to maintain a healthy spine.

Swimming, walking and cycling are still some of the best

general exercises, which will equip the body with greater strength and vitality. Sensible exercise speeds up circulation, strengthens the heart and keeps our arteries flexible. Exercises should be graded according to one's capacity, age and state of training and fitness. Consider how much better it is to have a game of tennis or squash instead of sitting in a pub, drinking alcohol or endangering our health with cigarettes!

The stimulation of physical exercising keeps the actions of the muscles smooth and serves the co-ordination of nerves and muscles — which is most important to keep our spine in good working order. In these modern times our bodies are often abused, as both mechanical and mental stress are considered to imbalance the spinal function.

The other day I again saw a patient who constantly seemed to 'put his back out', as he phrased it. In an effort to teach him how to relax I instructed him in the Hara breathing method. This method, by the way, is also described in detail in my book on *Stress and Nervous Disorders*. With this simple technique, natural suspension can be regained in the back. He was a grateful subject because he told me later that he felt able to correct his spine simply by following the guidelines of this breathing technique. There is a lot to be said for some of these self-help techniques, which when used sensibly and correctly can serve as an effective preventive method.

The main rule to any exercise programme is to start *slowly*. Always make sure that there are adequate warming-up and cooling-down periods, whatever programme one follows. With any kind of exercise, even breathing exercises, it is important to relax: avoid bouncing movements, especially when back problems exist. Muscles react like rubber bands and bouncing is never the ideal way to stretch a muscle.

Abdominal exercises could cause back strains and often weak backs can be traced back to a weakness in the abdominal muscular area. Any exertion that the stomach muscles cannot cope with results in strain on the back. Generally, my advice is that arching the lower back be avoided and that when lying on the floor the back should touch the floor wherever possible. If a suspected weakness exists in the back, never do straight leg sit-ups or leg-lifts.

Often, sprains are caused unnecessarily and to a lesser degree sprains are an injury, due to over-stretching. These are usually not associated with joint damage, but more frequently caused by over-use of a repeated sports movement in training or competition.

Symptoms can be acute and when, for instance, a rugby or soccer player is tackled, the sudden jerk can cause the player to feel an acute pain around the affected joint, which may be the result of a stretched ligament.

A sprain may involve the tearing of a muscle tendon or its attachment. Any ligament and tendon is prone to injury, especially when jerked suddenly, if not warmed up with the aid of massage and/or gentle exercise in advance.

Potential danger areas are always found in the hamstring muscles, the tendon behind the thigh bone, and in the quadriceps, the muscles found to the front of the thigh bone. The hamstrings are particularly vulnerable and in most cases the muscles in the back of the legs are not as flexible as they should be and so even more prone to damaged ligaments.

Any exercise programme should be built around the existing problem or weakness. There are specific exercises which can help back or neck problems. Many cases of pain in the lower-back area could be prevented by a correct posture and the following of a regular programme of abdominal exercises to increase flexibility.

In front of me lies a letter written by an elderly patient. She had previously sought my advice as to what she should or should not do in order to take care of her spine. I will quote part of the letter, which reads:

> When I saw you last, I was barely able to walk because of the severe pains in my back, leg and hip. Your advice has brought about a wonderful improvement. After eight days I knew the pain was diminishing and now I am free of pain in both leg and hip. I still have some pain left at the bottom area of my back, but have only myself to blame for this, as I have not yet quite found

the proper posture. I still find this rather difficult to remember and practise.

I will continue to follow your instructions and must tell you that it is three years since I have felt so well. All I can say is that words cannot express my gratitude.

I had advised this lady of some tips which I had picked up from my friend Dr Leonard Allan.

—Sleep on a firm mattress.
—On waking, stretch to loosen the muscles a bit before getting out of bed.
—Sit, stand and walk tall — improve the posture.
—Stay within your physical limitations and do not overdo any physical exercising.
—If you work in a cramped position, get up to stretch occasionally to loosen those cramped muscles.
—Are you trying to lift the load of two men? Don't — get some help.
—Does your work require you to bend excessively? If so, then always bend the legs and not the back.
—When bending, do not twist the spine, but keep it balanced.

With that advice, I am sure that even the remaining minor back problem which this lady still suffers will also disappear.

Another letter I have in front of me is from a younger person who seemed to be badly imbalanced in her walk. Although this had been apparent for quite some time, when she asked for my help I immediately realised that all that was needed was an adjustment to her left foot — the cuboid. One minor foot adjustment made sure that this young girl's walk completely reverted to normal.

Sometimes only a minor adjustment is needed. There was also the patient who wrote to me: 'How wonderful that after having suffered for so long, you managed to treat my trigeminal neuralgia so quickly.'

Normally I would have treated a case like hers with acupuncture or laser treatment. In her case, however, I applied acupressure with the thumb on the fossa at the angle of the jaw and instructed her to drink a half pint of distilled water every half hour. Simple adjustments and some back-up advice is often sufficient to end the suffering of some patients.

Another letter is from a patient who was frequently plagued by muscle spasms. Most muscle spasms can be eased by manipulation of the dorsal 10 and this person proved no exception. She responded to the treatment and her complaints became a thing of the past.

It makes me grateful to realise that such simple methods are available to us to ease often long-standing suffering. It encourages me to continue with the work I am doing daily and it is with the hope of minimising or eliminating unnecessary suffering that I have written this book.

I would like to finish with a quote from the book *Man — The Unknown*, written by Dr Alexis Carroll, which states: 'We are a nation of chronic invalids — because we have learned to suppress disease.'

Appendix

Exercises

Exercises for the lower back

NEVER OVERDO exercising, especially in the beginning. Start by trying the movements slowly and carefully. Do not be alarmed if the exercises cause some mild discomfort which lasts for a few minutes. If the pain is more than mild and lasts more than 15 or 20 minutes, *stop* and do no further exercises until you have seen your doctor.

Do the exercises on a hard surface covered with a thin mat or a heavy blanket. Put a pillow under your neck if it makes you more comfortable. Always start your exercises slowly and in the order given below, to allow the muscles to loosen up gradually. Heat treatments just before the start of the exercise programme can help to relax tight muscles. Follow the instructions carefully and it will be well worth the effort.

113

1. Stand erect while holding onto a table or chair. Bend knees, straighten up again, relax and repeat the exercise

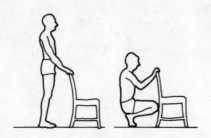

2. Lie on your back with your arms above your head and your knees bent. Now move one knee as far as you can towards your chest and at the same time straighten out the other leg. Go back to the original position with both knees bent and repeat the movements, switching legs. Relax and repeat the exercise

3. Lie on your back with your arms at your sides and your knees bent. Now bring your knees up to your chest and with your hands clasped, pull your knees towards your chest. Hold for a count of 10, keeping your knees together and your shoulders flat on the mat. Repeat the pulling and holding movement three times. Relax and repeat the exercise.

4. Lie on your back, grasp the right knee with both hands and pull the knee against the chest. Release the knee, then straighten it and relax. Repeat this exercise five times and then do the same thing with the left knee.

5. Bring one knee to the chest, then straighten it, pointing the toes upward as far as possible. Bend the knee back to the chest and return to original position. Alternate the knees with each repetition.

Do only one exercise, ten times per day, during an exercise session first thing in the morning: on the first day do exercise no. 1, on the second day exercise no. 2, etc. After doing the first five exercises for a couple of weeks, start on exercise no. 6, to be followed on successive days by nos. 7, 8 and 9. Following the same format then go back from exercise no. 9 to no. 1, again only one exercise per day.

6. With the knees bent, feet flat on the floor and hands clasped behind the head, pinch the buttocks together, pull in the abdomen and flatten the back against the floor. At first, hold this position for a count of five, relax for a further count of five, gradually increasing to counts of 20. Then do this same exercise with legs extended and arms raised straight overhead.

7. Sit on the floor with the knees bent. Keep the feet flat on the floor and held or hooked under a heavy piece of furniture, to provide leverage. Lie back and cross the arms on your chest, raise both head and shoulders and curl up to a sitting position. Keep the back rounded and pull with the abdominal muscles. Lower yourself slowly.

8. Lie face down, placing your hands on the lower back. Raise the head and shoulders (chest) from a prone position by contracting the back muscles (chin should be raised from the floor about 20 inches if possible). Hold this position for a count of five and return to starting position. Repeat this exercise five times.

9. Lie face down and place your hands and arms under the head. Contract the muscles of the lower back and legs by contracting the posterior extensors. Your feet should be raised to 20 inches above the floor. Hold this position for five seconds. Slowly return to starting position and repeat five times.

Helpful hints for a healthy back
Standing and walking:

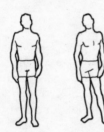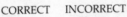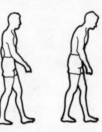

CORRECT   INCORRECT   CORRECT   INCORRECT

Point the toes straight forward when walking.
Place most of your weight on your heels.
Hold your chest forward and elevate the front of the pelvis as if walking up an incline.
Avoid wearing high heels.
Stand as if you are trying to touch the ceiling with the top of your head, eyes straight ahead.
All the elements of good posture will flow from these simple manoeuvres.

Sitting:

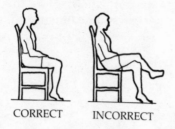

CORRECT   INCORRECT

Sit in a hard-back chair with the spine pushed back.
Try to eliminate the hollow in the lower back.
If possible, hold the knees higher than the hips while sitting in a car.
Secretaries should adjust their purpose-built chairs as required.
Sit all the way back in the chair, with your back straight.

Lifting:

CORRECT   INCORRECT

119

Bend your knees.
Bend and lift with your thigh muscles, *not* your back.
Never bend over with your knees straight and lift with the upper body.
Move slowly and avoid sudden movements.
Try to avoid lifting loads which are in front of you above the waistline.
Avoid bending forwards to lift heavy objects, from car boots for example, as this places a strain on the lower-back muscles.

Sleeping:

INCORRECT

CORRECT

Sleep on a firm mattress.
A ¾-inch plywood board under the mattress is useful under any circumstances, unless a firm orthopaedic mattress is used.
With acute back pain, sleep with a pillow or rolled-up blanket under the knees and a pillow under the head.
Keep your knees and hips bent when sleeping on your side.

Driving:

CORRECT   INCORRECT

Use a firm seat with a padded plywood or specially designed seat support.
Sit close to the wheel with the knees bent.
On long trips, stop every one or two hours and take a walk to relieve tension and relax the muscles.

Working:

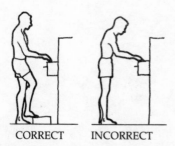

CORRECT   INCORRECT

Try to avoid fatigue caused by work requiring you to stand for long periods.
Flex the hips and knees by occasionally placing a foot on a stool or a bench.
Take exercise breaks from desk work by getting up, moving about and performing a few back exercises in the standing position.

121

Exercises for better back care
General instructions:

Your best back support is derived from your own back muscles! Regular and correct back exercises can often help to avoid the necessity of an external brace or corset. Back muscles can give you all the support needed if you strengthen them by the routine performance of prescribed exercises.

Follow the exercise routine prescribed by your doctor. Gradually increase the frequency of your exercises as your conditions improves, but stop when tired. If your arms are tight, take a warm shower or bath before performing your back exercises. Do not be alarmed if you feel a slight discomfort after having performed your exercises. This should diminish as your muscles become stronger.

Exercise on a rug or mat and put a small pillow under your neck. Wear loose clothing and remove any footwear. Stop doing any exercise which causes pain until you have checked with your doctor.

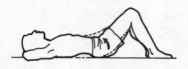

Lie on your back with knees bent and hands clasped behind the neck. Feet flat on the floor. Take a deep breath and relax. Press the small of your back against the floor and tighten the stomach and buttock muscles. This should cause the lower end of the pelvis to rotate forward and flatten the back against the floor.

Hold for five seconds and relax.

Lie on your back with knees bent and feet flat on the floor. Take a deep breath and relax. Clasp one knee with both hands and pull as close to the chest as possible. Return to starting position. Straighten your leg. Return to starting position. Repeat with the other leg.

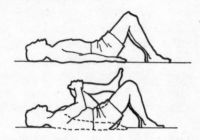

Lie on your back with knees bent and feet on the floor. Take a deep breath and relax. Grasp both knees and pull them as close to the chest as possible. Hold for three seconds, then return to starting position. Straighten the legs and relax.

Lie on your back with knees bent and feet flat on the floor. Take a deep breath and relax. Draw one knee to the chest; then point leg upward as far as possible. Return to starting position. Relax and repeat with the other leg.

This exercise is useful in stretching tight hamstring muscles, but is not recommended for those people with sciatic pain associated with a herniated disc.

a. Lie on your stomach with hands clasped behind the back. Pull the shoulders back and down by pushing hands downwards towards the feet, pinching the shoulder blades together. Lift your head from the floor. Take a deep breath and hold it for two seconds. Relax.

b. Stand erect. With one hand grasp the thumb of the other hand behind the back; then pull downwards towards the floor. Stand on the toes and look at the ceiling while exerting the downward pull. Hold momentarily and relax. Repeat this exercise ten times, at intervals of two hours, during the working day. Take an exercise break instead of a coffee break.

Stand with your back against the doorway. Place your heels four inches away from the frame. Take a deep breath and relax. Press the small of your back against the doorway.

Tighten your stomach and buttock muscles, allowing the knees to bend slightly. This should cause the lower end of the pelvis to rotate forward. Press the neck up against the doorway and press both hands against the opposite side of the doorway, straightening both knees. Hold for two seconds and relax.

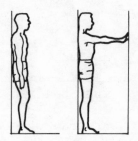

The following three exercises should not be started until you are free of pain and until the other exercises have been done for several weeks.

Lie on your back with your legs extended, knees unbent and arms at the sides. Take a deep breath and relax. Raise the legs one at a time as high as is comfortable and lower to the floor as slowly as possible.

Repeat five times for each leg.

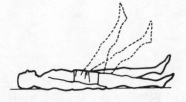

This exercise may be done with the help of a chair or a table. Bend in front of a chair or table and hold on to it. Flex the head forward, bounce up and down two or three times and then straighten out again.

125

Lie on your back with the knees bent. Feet flat on the floor. Take a deep breath and relax. Pull yourself up to a sitting position, keeping the knees bent. Return to starting position and relax.

Having someone hold your feet down on the floor facilitates this exercise.

Neck exercises
One of the causes of poor neck posture is muscle weakness. Certain exercises are especially useful for strengthening the muscles which maintain a good head and neck posture. Exercises alone will not cure your neck problems if you continue to put strain on your neck.

Incorrect posture:

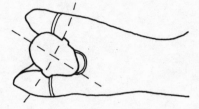

Avoid straining the neck at night in bed. If you lie on your back, puff up the pillow either side of your head, leaving a dent in the middle.

Correct posture:

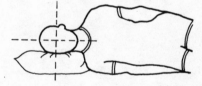

If you lie on your side, make sure that you have enough pillows to keep your head in a good position. At work, if you have a desk job or if you work at a bench, make sure that the working surface is the correct height for you, so that you do not have to bend down or stretch up to it.

Some simple exercises can be done while lying on the back with the knees bent and supported underneath by a pillow.

As a mobilising exercise: gently roll the head from side to side.

Slide your head down to one side, aiming the ear for the shoulder. Repeat the exercise on the other side.

Lift your head and try to look at your knees. Hold on for the count of five, put your head down and really relax.

Repeat these exercises ten times.

Sitting:

If you are sitting reading or watching television, make sure the book or television is in such a position that you do not have to look up at it by pushing the chin forward. Do not have them so low that the head hangs down on the shoulders.

Try to keep a good neck posture at all times and avoid falling asleep in the chair.

128

Correct position:

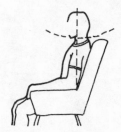

When doing the following exercise keep the shoulders stationary at all times and move only the head, slowly.

1. Bring chin to right shoulder.
2. Bring chin to left shoulder.
3. Drop head back — chin up.
4. Right ear to right shoulder, slowly stretch back.
5. Drop head forward — chin to chest.
6. Left ear to left shoulder, slowly stretch back.
7. Bring head back to centre.
8. Repeat, beginning with chin to left shoulder.

Shoulder exercises
Sit on a chair or the floor and let the arms hang loosely by the sides.

1. Circle the shoulders by shrugging shoulders up, drawing them back, then down and lastly forwards.

2. Touch the shoulders with the hands and draw circles with the elbows. Circle forwards ten times and then backwards ten times.

3. Keeping the back straight, stretch the arms:
   (a) out in front of the body;
   (b) out to the sides;
   (c) up in the air.

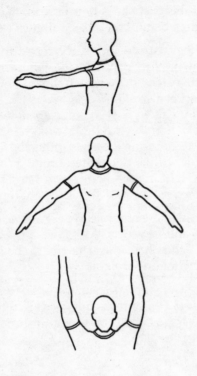

Try to touch your hands behind your neck and then try to touch your hands behind your back.

A variation of this exercise is to pass a small object behind your head and then behind your back. Repeat ten times.

Stand with the legs astride and lean over so that your arms hang loosely down. Now gently swing your arms out to the sides and try to reach further each time. This is called a pendular exercise. It also slightly separates the joint surfaces and so allows a little more movement. Repeat ten times.

A progression of this exercise is to swing the arms out to the sides and on the third swing the arms should be held out to the side for the count of five. Repeat ten times. Progress this by holding a 2 lb weight in each hand, increasing the weight as you become stronger.

Put one leg in front of the other, lean over as before. Swing the arms backwards and forwards. As before, progress by doing three swings and then hold the arms out to the count of five. Progress again by holding weights.

With legs apart, lean forward slightly with the arms slack alongside the body. Swing them outwards and bring them in again. Circle the hands about one foot out from the body in outward moving circles.

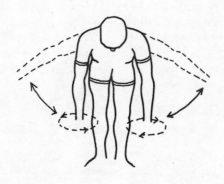

A very important exercise for anyone with a curvature of the spine

Stand against a door flattening the body into it. Bending the knees move up and down ten times. If support is needed a chair may be placed and held on to in front of you. Keep the spine as flat against the door as possible and the heels of the feet should also be pressed against the door.

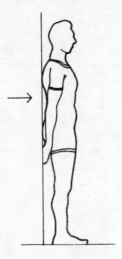

Exercise for easing the whole of the spine when in pain

Place two large pillows on the floor and lie face down with the pillows under the stomach area. Take a deep breath through the nose into the stomach. Imagine the stomach as a football and fill it with air. Then breathe out slowly through the mouth, like a steam engine.

Head exercise

Lie on a bed. The head, shoulders and arms should be allowed to hang down over the edge. Tuck the chin into the chest and make sure that there is no danger of falling off. Shake the head from left to right as if firmly refusing a request.

Keep this up for a few seconds and repeat this exercise several times per day. This exercise can also be done lying in bed and with an extra pillow placed under the shoulders.

Many problems will be alleviated by this exercise.

Sacro-iliac exercise

Try to do some gentle press-up exercises in a sitting position. It is best to use the edge of the bath for this exercise. Place the hands at the back of you on the edge of the bath with your bottom on the floor or on a low stool.

Keep the feet well in front of you on the floor so that your legs will not do the work for you. Push yourself up so that the bottom is not supported by the stool and then rest back on the stool again. Repeat this exercise five times.

133

Frozen shoulder exercises

Lie flat on your back with fingers clasped together. Raise the arms to an angle of 90 degrees, with straight elbows. Move up and down several times.

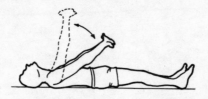

Lie flat on your back with fingers clasped together behind the neck. Pull the elbows in and then push out.

Using a strong towel, make movements as if drying your back. Gradually move the hands in closer.

Finally, some excellent advice always is to 'wear sensible shoes'!

Tension is an important factor in chronic backache. I must therefore stress the importance of the art of relaxation.

Never forget that no healing can take place unless total relaxation is obtained.

Bibliography

Peter John Hawkins, DO — *Osteopathic Diagnosis*, Tamo Pierston Publishers, 1985.

Carter Harrison Downing, DO — *Principles and Practice of Osteopathy*, Tamo Pierston Publishers, 1981.

Edythe F. Ashmore, DO — *Osteopathic Mechanics*, Tamo Pierston Publishers, 1981.

R. M. H. McMinn, R. T. Hutchings and B. M. Logan — *A Color Atlas of Head and Neck Anatomy*, Wolfe Medical Publications Ltd, London.

Denis Brookes, DO, PhD, MSO, MCO — *Cranial Osteopathy* Thorsons Publishers Ltd, Wellingborough, Northants.

Leon Chaitow, DO, ND — *Osteopathy*, Thorsons Publishers Ltd., Wellingborough, Northants.

Dr Muir Gray — *Football Injuries*, Publishers Offox Press, Oxford.

Laurie S. Hartman, DO, MRO — *Handbook of Osteopathic Technique*, Hutchinson, London.

Dr Ac. Leonard J. Allan, London — *Painless Pain Control, Body Energy Techniques*, L. J. Allen, Margate, Kent.

Prf. Dr Alfred Benninghoff — *Lehrbuch der Anatomie der Menschen*, J. F. Lehmans Verlag, München, Berlin, Germany.